CLARK MCGINN was born in Ayr and started talking at an early age. He's hardly stopped since. Educated at Ayr Academy and Glasgow University, he passed enough exams in-between speeches and debates to become a banker (in London and New York). He is happily married to Ann and currently lives in exile in Harrow-on-the-Hill. Since 1976 Clark has performed at Burns Suppers every year, delivering the Immortal Memory across the world, sharing his passion for the world's favourite poet.

In 2009, Burns's 250th anniversary year, Cl⌐⌐ President of The Burns Club of London (N⌐ ⌐⌐⌐ ⌐⌐⌐ ⌐⌐⌐⌐ ns Federation) and gave the Addres⌐ ⌐⌐⌐ ⌐⌐⌐ ⌐ Service in Westminster Abbey on ⌐

Luath has also publishe⌐ ⌐⌐⌐ ⌐⌐⌐ 'cottish and *The Luath Kilmarnock* ⌐⌐⌐ ⌐⌐⌐ ⌐⌐cu the Afterword), and his insider's viev ⌐⌐⌐ ⌐⌐⌐ ⌐⌐al crisis, *Out of Pocket: How collective amnesia lost ↓↓e world its wealth, again.*

The Ultimate Burns Supper Book

*A Practical (but Irreverent) Guide
to Scotland's Greatest Celebration*

This Book Contains Everything You Need
To Enjoy or Arrange a Burns Supper –

Just Add Food, Drink and Friends

CLARK McGINN

Luath Press Limited

EDINBURGH

www.luath.co.uk

First published 2006
Reprinted 2007
New revised edition 2010
Reprinted 2012
Reprinted 2013
Reprinted 2015
Reprinted 2016
Reprinted 2017
Reprinted 2021

ISBN: 978-1-906817-50-3

The paper used in this book is recyclable. It is made from
low chlorine pulps produced in a low energy, low emissions
manner from renewable forests.

FSC
www.fsc.org
FSC® C023367
The mark of
responsible forestry

Printed and bound by
Robertson Printers, Forfar

Illustrations © A. Martin Pittock

Typeset in 10.5pt Sabon by
3btype.com

Acknowledgements

To Ann. Full Stop.

At least, that's what I'd always promised myself I would write as a dedication if ever one of my writing projects actually got published, thus avoiding the 'there are too many people to thank: Mrs Mackay, Mrs Macleod for her cakes…' school of thanksgiving.

Then the temptation came to add a quip and my children, so it became:

To Ann, who feeds my sporran with milk and my ego with regularity, without whom this would not have happened, and to Claire, Eleanor and Emma, without whom this extra job would not be necessary. Then my Mum (who had the good sense to deliver me in Burns's home of Ayrshire). But what about William Reid, my Rector at Ayr Academy, who gave me my first booking in 1976? Or the University of Glasgow (both the institution and its people) who taught me the way, the truth and the life? I can't leave out Glasgow University Union, the pre-eminent student debating union in the world, whose training allowed me to win the *Observer* Mace and whose ethos gave me the earth to plant the seed that grew into the World Student Debating Competition. The Union also gave me my partnerships with Jimmy, Liam and Charles, and their friendship. Not forgetting the English-Speaking Union. I, like so many others, am truly grateful to them for providing the opportunities and experience of the us Debating Tour, in my case happily with Mark. Of course, as always, I think of my good friends (who have heard the stories so many times before) and give especial thanks to Murray for providing the big picture and to Anne for drawing the wee pictures. My thanks, too, to Gavin, Cat and the Luath team.

Have I forgotten anyone? I could pad this out, but will reduce it to one last category and one last person: thank you to the relatively many people in the audience who have laughed at the relatively few jokes and thanks to Dad (as RB would have described him: 'A gentleman who held the patent of his honours directly from Almighty God') who, in his combined roles as a freemason and caterer probably saw more haggises addressed than any man alive.

Thank you.

Clark McGinn

Brief Thoughts On A Second Edition

Thank you to everyone who has made suggestions and comments about new ideas and old traditions that can help make a Burns Supper even more fun.

As we approach the end of Homecoming Year marking the 250th anniversary of RB's birth in 1759, more people than ever before, in more countries than Burns could have imagined, have joined in the fun of the Burns Supper.

The explosive growth of folk joining in over the last decade is largely because we've realised that you can hold a great party with friends to celebrate the life and works of Scotland's national poet in almost any size or shape of event – there isn't a one-size-fits-all Burns night. I believe that the key ingredients are toasting Burns, sharing a Haggis and enjoying his songs and poems: everything else should match the people attending. Burns had a chameleon character which appealed to peasants and nobles, to rich and poor, to professors of the Scottish Enlightenment and bar room philosophers. His birthday party should be equally eclectic.

Enjoy it!

Clark McGinn Dec 2009

Contents

Here's a bottle and an honest friend!
What wad ye wish for mair, man?
Wha kens, before his life may end,
What his share may be o' care, man?

Then catch the moments as they fly,
And use them as ye ought, man;
Believe me, happiness is shy,
And comes not aye when sought, man.[1]

---

[1] *'A Bottle and an Honest Friend.'*

Foreword

BURNS SUPPERS HAVE BEEN in existence for over 200 years, and there are probably more taking place now than at any time in their history. They are a unique phenomenon: the celebration of the life and work of a poet by companies, societies, schools and families across the globe. Some folk are dismissive of them, and some are protective of them, making them sound difficult and only for time-served Scots or those of Scots descent. Both groups are wrong. Burns aimed to speak for everyone who appreciates the fact that 'the best-laid plans of mice and men' are not to be relied on, the sad truth that 'Man's inhumanity to man / Makes thousands mourn', the deep feeling of 'My love is like a red, red rose', or the sheer unwillingness so many have experienced on having to leave a pub at closing time. No other poet is celebrated across the world as Burns is, so he succeeded in that aim. He has over 1,000 clubs and societies dedicated to him; his books have been translated 3,000 times into more than 50 languages. Every Burns Supper has an Immortal Memory, because that is what each of them is: an immortal memorial to 'Ranting, roving Robin'.

As that name Burns gave himself suggests, though, Burns Suppers are not meant to be po-faced affairs, but parties of good fellowship, where the speeches are short, the pleasure long, and we may be briefly 'o'er all the ills of life victorious'. Holding a Burns Supper is easy and fun, and holding the Ultimate Burns Supper isn't too difficult either. Not everyone who reads this book will want to hold an Ultimate Burns Supper every time, but after reading it, I can guarantee they will be able to hold one any time.

Clark McGinn, the author of this book, is one of the foremost Burns Supper speakers in the UK. But more to the point, he is also a peerless host and extremely experienced in Burns evenings of every kind, from the celebrations of hundreds to family occasions. We may not all have his energy, his wit or his verve, but here they are in print: an unfailing source of reference, a pocket guide to everything from neeps to sporrans, alike informed by his Ayrshire roots and adult experience of the Burns circuit in England, the US and elsewhere. Read Clark's book and you will know what was wrong if you've ever been to a boring Burns Supper organised by someone else, and you'll also make sure you never have a dull moment at one run by yourself. This is the best, the clearest, the sharpest, the only guide you will ever need.

Robert Burns is a global poet, an excuse for a worldwide party, and a major tourist business. When David Stenhouse of BBC Scotland commissioned World Bank Economist Lesley Campbell to conduct research on how much 'Burns the Brand' is worth to the Scottish economy, the answer was £157.25 million. If your Burns Supper is a corporate event, it's not only a party: it's a contribution to a continuing and growing business. Yours of course, but also that of Robert Burns.

Enjoy this book: you'll laugh out loud – at least I did, and I've heard all the jokes before. Enjoy your Burns Supper: it will be better fun than ever after this. Enjoy Burns and his poetry, which, like his appeal, lives after him. A toast to all who buy this book to celebrate the Immortal Memory of Robert Burns.

Murray Pittock
Bradley Professor of English Literature and Dean of the Faculty
*   of Arts, The University of Glasgow*

SECTION ONE

The History

'Vehement Celebrations' – Why do we bother in the first place?

There was a lad was born in Kyle,
But whatna day o' whatna style,
I doubt it's hardly worth the while,
To be sae nice wi' Robin[2,3]

SO – YOU HAVE BEEN invited to a Burns Supper, maybe for the first time, perhaps for the fiftieth – but what is it all about?

The first Burns Supper was held in 1801 just a few years after Burns's death and since then the number of people – Scots and 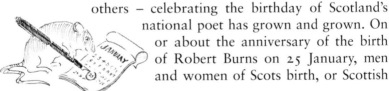 others – celebrating the birthday of Scotland's national poet has grown and grown. On or about the anniversary of the birth of Robert Burns on 25 January, men and women of Scots birth, or Scottish

---

[2] *All of the epigraphs to the chapters following come from the poems of Robert Burns – and I've chosen them to illustrate the theme, so they make excellent quotations on invitations, menus and the like (see Appendix V, too). (Where the title is the same as a song's first line, I haven't bothered to add a footnote.) Epigraphs were important to RB, too – please see Prof Murray Pittock's 2004 Chatterton Lecture 'Robert Burns and British Poetry' (published in* Proceedings of the British Academy *121, 191–211).*

[3] *'There was a Lad'.*

descent, who are alumni of Scots universities and schools, who serve in Scottish regiments[4] or work for Scottish companies, who play golf, who like poetry, who revere Burns, who respect freedom and human spirit, who have a fondness for Scotland, who like wholesome food and good drink, who need little excuse for a party in good company; all these people meet in congregations from three or four to over a thousand folk, to celebrate the life, the works and the philosophy of Robert Burns.

Without a doubt, this is unique. There are no other spontaneous celebrations of poetry in the world,[5] while only one other historical figure (Lord Nelson[6]) receives the accolade of an annual toast to his 'Immortal Memory'[7] (albeit on the anniversary of his glorious death, rather than of his humble birth). This personal cult is occasionally attacked by a school of academia that sees it as unstructured sentimental gush, but that's flying in the face of a storm. Many speakers at Burns Suppers enlighten us, while many performers illuminate the words of the poems and songs. It is a great and, in the best of both senses, popular tradition.

The best book about the history and development of the Burns Supper is John Cairney's *Immortal Memories*[8] and his extensive collection of speeches and stories is pretty definitive. So, the next question must be, 'even if the Burns Supper is important – why another book?'

---

[4] *This was written in the plural just before the foolhardy reforms to amalgamate all of Scotland's infantry regiments into one.*

[5] *Although the Finns hold a holiday on 5 February, the birthday of Johan Ludvig Runeburg, their national poet.*

[6] *Vice Admiral Horatio, Viscount Nelson, the victor of the great naval battle of Trafalgar in 1805 which won command of the seas for Britain in the wars against Napoleon.*

[7] *At Trafalgar Dinners each year on 21 October, the anniversary of his victory and death at the battle of Trafalgar.*

[8] *John Cairney,* Immortal Memories, *Luath Press, 2003.*

Fair point, dear Reader (though if you're reading this it's odds-on you've bought the blessed thing – but let's pretend you haven't for a couple of minutes).[9]

Many, upon receiving their first invitation to a Burns Supper, think of the upcoming event as a cold, boring, formal dinner-jacketed lecture where an elderly, male audience (suitably[10] lubricated by whisky) performs unintelligible traditional rituals to the sound of the bagpipes. This is enough to put many off – but unfairly. There are many ways to commemorate Burns and to enjoy a Burns Night – which should be a synonym for good food, good drink and good company arranged to celebrate the genius of the poet.

If a Burns Supper is about anything, it is about capturing the vital spark that Burns left and, for an evening at least, living with a greater insight into what it is not just to be Scottish, but to be human.

I hope that this book will do two things:

1   Explain, for those of you who are going to your first Burns Night (and for those who've been many times before, and still wonder about some aspect or other of the proceedings), the whys and hows of the evening, helping you enjoy your attendance by de-mystifying the events you will see and share in, *and*

2   Give practical advice, without preaching,[11] to those of

---

9   *Or at least I hope that, after drinking your skinny double caramel latte in the big comfy chair in the popular book chain, you'll feel guilty enough to buy this on the way out!*

10   *Or unsuitably?*

11   *Much…*

you prompted (or delegated) to arrange a Burns Supper (whether for four or 400, in a hall or at home) and to those due to speak, recite, sing or perform.

In each case, I hope the end result will be a truly enjoyable and memorable evening.

Is this small volume definitive? No! But I have been travelling on the Burns road since addressing my first haggis in 1976 at Ayr Academy. So after thirty years I feel like Sergio McLeone – I know the Good, the Bad and the Ugly when it comes to Burns Suppers. That's what I want to share with you – one Ayrshireman's experiences and suggestions – in the hope that you'll enjoy your party (however big or small) all the more. When studying at Glasgow, my Professor, Robin Downie, taught me about 'The Adam Smith Problem' – which arises out of Adam Smith's two greatest works: *An Inquiry Into The Nature And Causes Of The Wealth of Nations* and *The Theory Of Moral Sentiments*. The former is known as the bible of capitalism but the latter shows a common sense and communitarian approach to morality based on his concept of sympathy. How could one author believe both? Because the first is *descriptive* of the world today as we pass through it and try to make sense of it; the second is *prescriptive* of how we should run the world tomorrow. This therefore is a merely descriptive book.[12] If some of the ideas strike a chord remember them. If none do, abuse them.

But in any case – whether as guest, entertainer or arranger – this will help you enjoy your own Burns Supper.

There are many traditions, accidents and quirks which make up anyone's idea of the great Burns Supper, and so there are many points of disagreement and rival procedures or formats. I, for

---

[12] *If you are looking for a prescription, ask a pharmacist.*

one, am glad that it is important enough to us to generate these controversies and novelties. I think this tradition of conflicting approaches is why Walt Whitman called Burns Night the 'vehement celebrations'.[13]

Since 2000, about half my Immortal Memories have been given outside the UK (mainly in the USA, but also in Europe, the Middle East and Australia), where sometimes no one has been to a Burns Supper before – and one of the great happinesses I have is seeing those guests come back a second or third time to share in our big Burns party.

Robert Burns is worthy of remembrance: as a poet, first and foremost; as a man who faced the challenges and difficulties of life; as the National Bard of Scotland (whatever that might mean); and in many other contexts. I have been honoured to speak in many different countries and there has never been a time when the members of the audience, 'the folk in the body of the kirk', be they Burnsians or novices, Scots or foreigners, literary or drunk, haven't thought for a moment, reflected on the truth, and seen something in their own lives or in the world opened up by the words and the immortal poetry of Robert Burns.

In a world of haste and thoughtlessness that's no bad thing.

---

[13] *Walt Whitman*, Prose Works, *Harvard Classics, 1892 – Part V 'November Boughs', 7: 'Robert Burns as Poet and Person'. Given Whitman's great gifts as a poet, this article is praise indeed.*

The History of the Burns Supper – How did we get here?

I lang hae thought, my youthfu' friend,
A something to have sent you,
Tho' it should serve nae ither end
Than just a kind memento:
But how the subject-theme may gang,
Let time and chance determine:
Perhaps it may turn out a sang;
Perhaps, turn out a sermon.[14]

After the sermon of the first section, let us join in the song of the Burns Supper. The aim of this small book is not to set rules or precepts on how a Burns Supper *must* be held, but to give an introduction to the many parts for those who are unfamiliar; to add a few side swipes at many who believe themselves 'expert'; and to help you have an enjoyable and memorable evening in conjunction with the hundreds of thousands of folk across the globe who celebrate the Burns Supper.

---

14   *'Epistle to a Young Friend'.*

The very first supper, held in Burns Cottage itself in 1801, saw nine 'honest men' of Ayr sit at table.[15] With a simple genius, the Reverend Hamilton Paul, who organised the celebration, hit on all of the key ingredients which we still see today:

- **Addressing the Haggis** – and a big bowl of haggis, neeps an' tatties for all.
- The Toast to the **Immortal Memory** of Robert Burns.
- Good **food,** plenty of **drink** and convivial **company.**
- **Recitation** and **celebration** of the works of our poet.

Within a few years the great and ancient Burns Clubs grew across Scotland – originally at Greenock and Paisley[16] – and within ten years, the Burns Supper was a common January occurrence in cities, towns, corporations and institutions, Masonic lodges and church halls. Over the years many barnacles have become attached to the Supper Ship but I feel that you and your mate could form a perfectly canonical Burns Night eating haggis

-----

[15] *These nine gentlemen, all personally acquainted with Burns, were: Hamilton Paul; John Ballantyne (The Provost of Ayr); 'Orator Bob' Aitken; William Crawford (who had employed RB's father); Patrick Douglas (who found RB a potential job in Jamaica); Primrose Kennedy; David Scott (the banker involved in settling the dispute on the Lochlie farm); Hew Fergusson (Barrackmaster); and Thomas Jackson, the Rector of Ayr Academy (where a Burns Supper is still held every January). There is a popular misconception that one of the original guests was a woman – but I assure you that Primrose Kennedy was a man (albeit quaintly named). That being said, a mixed Burns Supper is the norm outside a handful of the ancient and specialist clubs. The first dinner was on the anniversary of RB's death, 21 July, but the second dinner was held in January 1802.*

[16] *Or perhaps Paisley and Greenock – there's a lot of debate on who is oldest – especially in Greenock and Paisley.*

suppers[17] in a chippie off the Gallowgate in Glasgow with two cans of Tennents to wash them down. (The wee chippie man might get a bit worried about the addressing knife – but if you're relatively discrete you should manage to escape a night in the Glasgow Constabulary's hospitality.)[18]

The single, most important purpose of the Burns Supper is to bring enjoyment in the spirit of Burns's life and poems. So here are the only three precepts I would lay down to guide you through this short and helpful book:

- Have as many or as few people as you want to invite.
- Have as much food and drink as you can afford.
- Have as much or as little formality as you all feel comfortable with. (But don't forget a haggis, a poem and a toast to RB!)

In the next section, we will look at Burns's life, after which the plan is to go through a typical Burns Supper in chronological order – from sending out or receiving the invitations, to the proceedings of the night both in terms of the dinner and the entertainment. At the end we will look at smaller suppers and ways to adapt the format to any shape or size of company.

So with those ground rules, as they say in Glasgow: 'Let's get tore in'...

---

[17] *Deep fried of course.*

[18] *Though as the Strathclyde Police Pipe Band is one of the finest bands that I've had the pleasure of performing with, you might be lucky and have a considerate bandsman take you in.*

The Man Himself

For me, I'm on Parnassus' Brink,
Rivin' the words to gar them clink;
Whyles daez't wi' love, whyles daez't wi' drink
  Wi' jads or Masons,
An' whyles, but ay owre late I think,
  Braw sober lessons.[19]

This is the most difficult chapter as I want to give a short biography of the phenomenon we know as Robert Burns. I logged on to Amazon to see how many books on, and biographies of, RB were in print – an extraordinary 5,385! And each has a slightly different view. There's the

- Plowman/Poet/Radical/Wha Daur Meddle Wi' Me School.
- Demon Lover/Drinker/Writer School.
- Romantic/Lay Me Doon an' Die School.
- National Bard of Scots Wha Hae School.

Which is the true reflection of the man and his works? That is one of the appeals and challenges of Burns – each of us needs to take time and thought (whether by listening to Immortal Memories or reading or discussing) to reach our own view of his many facets. But that's secondary – the first and most important thing is the immediacy, the initial appeal of his poems.

This brief outline of RB's life is too short and my excuse (believe it or not) is that I've endeavoured to make sure that everyone feels it's insufficient. Maybe that will encourage you to find out more!

---

[19] *'To Davie – Second Epistle'.*

1759   In Alloway, beside Ayr, on 25 January, in a small clay-walled, thatched cottage, Robert Burns is born to a Kincardineshire gardener and his wife – William Burnes[20] and Agnes Brown Burnes. Over time, the family grows to four boys and three girls.

1765   William, in the self-help tradition still popular in Scotland, hires a young schoolmaster, John Murdoch, to teach RB and his younger brother, Gilbert. They spend three years under his care. (RB may have been a 'ploughman poet' but don't ever assume that he was uneducated.) RB attends school off and on over the coming years.

1766   In an attempt to expand his business, William decides to give up the market garden beside the cottage and become a tenant farmer. He rents Mount Oliphant farm (this proves to be a disastrous choice). Robert and Gilbert are needed to work the farm but William teaches them himself while RB enjoys his mother's singing of old Scots songs and rhymes.

1772   Murdoch returns to Ayr to teach at Ayr Academy[21] and RB joins him for three weeks, mastering Grammar, helping in a dramatic production, and learning basic French.

         This year's harvest sees RB working the fields beside an older girl, Nellie, who has been given a poem by

---

[20] *William spelled his family name in the Northern fashion. Robert changed to 'Burns' in 1785 in line with Ayrshire orthography.*
[21] *Still in existence today, the Academy is the oldest school in Scotland, founded before 1233.*

another boy. RB trumps this offering in his first poem, 'Handsome Nell'.

1774/76   Mount Oliphant yields little as a farm – hardly enough to keep the Burnes family alive. The hard work and privation begin to tell on William Burnes, and many think that these years took their toll on RB's health as well.

1777   William has the opportunity to break the lease at Mount Oliphant as a neighbour wants to increase his farm. The family move to a new tenancy at Lochlea.

1779/80   While the first farm was in the back of beyond, Lochlea is near the rather cheerful town of Tarbolton, easily within reach for the older Burnes children. RB enjoys the company in the various taverns (probably exaggerating the amount he drinks).[22] In defiance of his father's wishes he joins a dancing class and founds a drinking and debating club called 'The Tarbolton Bachelors Club'. The following year sees him join the more mature surroundings of the Freemasons[23] (where he rises to be the Depute Master of St James Lodge Tarbolton).

1781   RB has his first formal courting – Alison Begbie, for whom he writes three songs, including 'Mary Morison'. Alison, perhaps wisely, enjoys his poetics but nothing else.

---

[22] *'Probably' – in his letters to his acquaintances it's hard to tell where braggadocio begins – a running problem for all of his biographers.*

[23] *Ayrshire is the home of the foundation of modern Freemasonry (Lodge No 0, Mother Kilwinning).*

Later this year, William's bad luck continues as his landlord disputes how they should share the burden of paying for some capital expenditure. This dispute drags through the courts and hastens his death.

1781   RB is sent away to learn flax dressing to establish himself in trade. The project is a failure – although RB wins an award for the quality of his work, he finds Irvine uncongenial[24] and has a first bout of depression. New Year's Day 1782 sees the flax shop burn down as one of the drunks sets fire to the store room. RB returns to his family home, where the atmosphere and the harvest are equally stretched.

1783   In an *annus horribilis*, the legal processes grind and grind. Robert and Gilbert take on more of the running of the farm as William is obviously dying. In April, RB starts his *Commonplace Book* – noting, working and developing his poetry amongst all the stress and strain. The position at Lochlea is untenable, whichever way the court case goes. Robert and Gilbert see the need to have a 'Plan B' and so rent the farm of Mossgeil for the three months hence.

1784   Good news/Bad news.

In January Scotland's highest court finds in favour of William. Two weeks later he is dead and the remaining family leaves the hateful fields of Lochlea. The brothers start to work the new farm.

1785   'Rab Mossgeil', as he styles himself, becomes known around the countryside and towns as 'different' – his Tarbolton flirting takes on a new turn with the birth of

---

[24] *And that was before the town was 'redeveloped' in the 1970s…*

Elizabeth, his illegitimate daughter by Elizabeth Paton his family's farm servant. 'Dear Bought Bess' causes RB many problems with the local Church, but he and his mother take the child into the family. This is the first of RB's many children.[25]

1785   In the midst of all this, RB meets Jean Armour, who is to be the love of his life, and – against her parents' wishes – she and Robert declare themselves married.[26] Now RB's life begins to get complicated.

Old Mr Armour throws a fit, as do the Minister and all the good folk of Ayrshire. Even RB's friends seem keen to disentangle the newlyweds and the document they signed together is mutilated, with their names cut out.

1786   *Annus mirabilus*!

The temperature increasing, RB meets with a sea-captain friend who suggests he emigrate to Jamaica to escape the furore. RB arranges a job (on a slave plantation) and

---

[25] *There is some uncertainty over the exact number of children RB fathered, but the consensus is twelve bairns by four women. It is very important to know that (with one lapse which was rectified) he was a good father and met his parental responsibilities to both the babies and the women.*

[26] *Until the Marriages (Scotland) Act 1939, as well as through a formal church service, in Scotland marriage could be effected in a number of so-called 'irregular' but strictly legal ways. One, by declaration without parental consent* (marriage de presenti), *gave rise to the popularity of Gretna Green as a wedding locale, as Lord Hardwicke's Act 1753, had made parental approval mandatory for young people in England. Another form was where a man had promised to marry a woman and on the strength of that promise, they had had sex* (promise subsequente copula). *The final form of irregular marriage ('by habit and repute') was only abolished in 2005.*

agrees with the Armours that he and Jean will repudiate each other. This they do and RB is certified a single man by the Kirk. (The fact that Jean is pregnant is not yet known.)

To raise the cash to pay his fare, he sends his poems to a printer in Kilmarnock, who likes them and undertakes to publish a small edition of 36 poems, including 'To A Mouse' and 'The Holy Fair'.

Between April and May RB meets 'Highland Mary' Campbell, falling in love on the rebound from Jean and – possibly – agreeing to marry her. A great, short love – the details are very obscure. It ends sadly as Mary dies of a fever later in the year in Greenock,[27] causing RB to write 'To Mary in Heaven' and possibly also 'Flow Gently Sweet Afton'.

In July, Old Man Armour threatens legal proceedings against the father of his soon to be born grandchildren and so Robert goes into hiding, transferring his half of Mossgiel into Gilbert's name and the copyright of his poems to his baby daughter to avoid the lawyers.

31 July sees the publication of 612 copies of *Poems, Chiefly in the Scottish Dialect* – known to us as *The Kilmarnock Edition*. This edition sells quickly.

Everything changes!

Burns delays his departure for Jamaica, while Jean is delivered of a boy and a girl.

Critical acclaim throughout Scotland leads RB to Edinburgh in November – Edinburgh is at its peak as an intellectual hub and Burns meets and shares in the intellectual life of the capital.

---

[27] *There are many controversies about this period in RB's life – was Mary pregnant when she died? The discussions rumble on.*

1787   The turn of the year sees him proclaimed 'Caledonia's Bard', with a second edition of the poems to be published in Edinburgh. This edition includes the first book publication of the 'Address to a Haggis'.

RB tours Scotland (with a brief foray onto English soil), being welcomed into the homes of the great and the good, falling in love with an Edinburgh girl, Peggy Chalmers (unusually unrequited, as it happens).

He starts collecting songs and renovating for the great work *Scots Musical Museum*, which will see the preservation of much of Scotland's song heritage.

1788   Back in Edinburgh RB enters into correspondence and an amour with Mrs Agnes 'Nancy' Maclehose – he signing 'Sylvander', she 'Clarinda'. A bad knee injury, combined with some vestigial moral awareness on the part of Clarinda, leaves this unconsummated (RB impregnates her maid called Jenny Clow instead. Jean is carrying twins, too, though both die within weeks of birth).

In February, he returns to Tarbolton publically and confirms that Jean is his wife. He looks at Ellisland Farm and takes it to support his family,[28] while planning to obtain a government salary as an excise man by using the influence of his new Edinburgh connections.

The Kirk recognise the marriage between RB and Jean and Burns takes up the life of a farmer, excise officer

---

[28]   *RB's friend John Tennant of Glenconnor helped them find Ellisland. I met his great-granddaughter in 1983 – Lady Elliot of Harwood (who was 80 and whose father was 87 when she was born). She told me of the family tales of Burns, especially that he had a 'keen and burning eye that you would never forget'.*

and family man while collating songs and lyrics for the *Musical Museum*.

1789/92 RB's health begins a slow decline, but his family increases – two sons and a daughter for Jean and one more illegitimate child.

Farming is difficult, but Burns is making a good name in the government service, although there is an uncertainty about his liberal politics as the continent reels under the French Revolution. He clears his name, pretty much, and works hard, though the household budget is tough.

Burns gives up Ellisland after a hard slog and decamps with Jean and the children to Dumfries, where he is promoted. He starts collaborating on a second collection of Scottish songs and writes his greatest work, 'Tam o' Shanter'.

1793/95 He continues his excise work diligently (rising to Acting Supervisor) and, for no pay, is the guiding light behind the *Select Scottish Airs* project, which makes yet further strides in the saving of Scotland's precious folk song heritage. His temperament causes foolish breaches with old friends, Mrs Dunlop and the Riddells. Jean has another son.

While it is obvious that RB is still fond of a drink, he is not the alcoholic that is sometimes described.[29] His health is, however, failing.

---

[29] *Burns is often castigated for his enjoyment and over-enjoyment of a dram, but it must be seen in context to avoid hypocrisy. William Pitt the Younger, who was born in the same year as Burns, was Prime Minister for the second longest period in British history and is said to have consumed three bottles of port each and every evening and was certainly an alcoholic at the time of his death in 1806.*

1796   Rheumatic fever sets in and affects him seriously. Cold sea baths are prescribed[30] but the early strain of his farming life takes its toll and, looked after by Jean, who is again nine months pregnant and assisted by pretty Jenny Lewars (the object of RB's final gentle flirting), Robert Burns dies at the Mill Vennel house (now Burns Street) in Dumfries on 21 July.

He is buried with full civic and military[31] honours four days later, just as Jean gives birth to their last child.

These are the bare bones of a complex and complicated life. There are many uncertainties and many controversies but this is not the place to air them. I leave you will a simple thought – look at his legacy, not his history.

Let's move on quickly to explore that legacy and how we celebrate it in practice in the Burns Supper.

---

[30] *I'm not a doctor, but this doesn't in hindsight seem such a good idea.*

[31] *The Captain of the Soldiers was the future Lord Liverpool, Prime Minister of the UK.*

SECTION TWO

The Burns Supper

Before You Sit Down

Invitations

SIR,

Yours this moment I unseal,
   And faith I'm gay and hearty!
To tell the truth and shame the deil,
   I am as fou as Bartie:
But Foorsday, sir, my promise leal
   Expect me o' your partie,
If on a beastie I can speel,
   Or hurl in a cartie.

YOURS,

ROBERT BURNS
MAUCHLINE, *Monday night, 10 o'clock*[32]

Probably the first thought of attending a Burns Supper comes when the invitation falls on the doormat (or e-mail inbox). What to do? What to expect?

On the other side of the equation, if you are the lucky organiser, after you have decided where to hold your Burns Supper and have drawn up your guest list (small or large), the next step is to send out the invitations. I say 'send out', but you can call people and ask them to come round if you want. However, the fun of

---

[32] *'A Versified Reply to an Invitation'* – *'Bartie' is the Devil!*

receiving an invitation is hard to beat and it begins to get everyone in the mood for a celebration.

Here we are looking at the general invitation; entertainers and speakers (and Guests of Honour) will expect and require a more personal approach – so write a letter or e-mail, or even better call them up to discuss the evening.

What should a good invitation look like?

Amongst the Duke and Earls and anyone entitled to wear Eagle Feathers in his cap[33] I'm sure that formal, gold edged and engraved pasteboard is *de rigueur*. For a larger dinner often it will be a flyer or prospectus (with the details of the venue, entertainment and cost, incorporating a way of replying and paying – key advice: always get the money upfront), followed by an entry ticket. It's good to have a Burns motif on these: typically it will be a drawing or silhouette of Rabbie's head, but I have seen Burns Cottage or the Burns Monument or just a tartan border.

For a family party, many stationers sell blank party invitations for Burns Suppers – the only effort needed is to have the family member whose handwriting least looks like that of a doctor with the DTs fill in the blanks. Or you can be more inventive. My Wife-and-Partner-in-the-Dance and I have used:

---

[33] *Just so you don't commit a* faux pas, *you shouldn't get into the habit of carrying large feathers in your hat. You might be unlucky and bump into some militant bird watching activist who will spray you with red paint, or possibly (but even more unlikely) some Highland Chief could challenge you to a duel on the basis of your false claim to be a Somebody – three feathers indicate a clan chief; two the head of a family; and you are allowed one if you have your own coat of arms with the Lord Lyon in Edinburgh. Just so you know! (Any ordinary Joe does have the right to wear the clan badge – usually the chief's crest within a circular, stylised belt and buckle, with a sprig of the clan's plant as a marker.)*

- **Miniatures of Malt Whisky** – either empty (where the whisky has been used for puddings)[34] with the invitation inside the bottle, or full with a label tied on with tartan ribbon, as in the famous *Alice In Wonderland* episode ('Drink Me!' on one side and the invitation on the other).

- **The Recipe for the Haggis** (highly suitable in litigious societies where the fainthearted might sue when they hear what's inside the haggis – prior disclosure is an effective legal protection!)

- A picture of **Sir Harry Lauder** ironing his kilt (it seemed like a good idea at the time).

- Copies of **Tintin's Scottish adventure** *The Black Isle*.

- A 45 rpm record of **'Donald Where's Your Troosers'** (with the invite stuck on the sleeve).[35]

- **Postcards** – we've used the UK Post Office's cards with Burns Poems, and pictures of Rabbie, Burns Cottage, Ayrshire scenes and even haggises.

- **E-cards** – there are a number of good sites with specific Burns themes or general haggis and Scotland images.

---

[34] *That's my story and I'm sticking to it!*

[35] *This one nearly got me into trouble – the single was reissued in 1992 in an attempt to (a) become the Christmas No 1 in the UK charts and (b) prop up the late, great Andy Stewart's pension in his old age. The record shop I visited to buy 40 copies was one of the reporting units and I was taken aside under suspicion of Chart Rigging…*

- RBS Houston sent a card with a **piper** on the front and a wheel on the back which let you change the tartan of his kilt to match yours!

- You could use a nice invitation card and stick a 250th Anniversary postage stamp at the top as a motif.

But you get the idea.

As a recipient, please make sure that you reply to the invitation in good time to help your host/arranger calculate the numbers and fix the seating plan.

The next big question is what to write by way of invitation. I know that you're getting bored of the two schools of thought approach, so I'll make up a third one in this case.

Version One: 'The Name, Rank and Serial Number'

This gives just the basic details – handwritten or typed. The key data the audience/guests need are:

- when and where,
- time of kick-off (and you might consider an end time – some people like one, to help with planning babysitters etc.) and
- How to dress (if clothes are required; let's not make censorious assumptions).

To Walter and Scott

What though on hamely fare we dine,
Wear hoddin grey, an' a that;
Gie fools their silks, and knaves their wine;
A Man's a Man for a' that:

Ann and Clark hope you will come to their

BURNS SUPPER

On

Saturday 25 January

At Home at 7.30 for 8.00 pm[36]

RSVP[37] to annandclark@ultimateburns.com
Dress: Come as you are, but wear something tartan!

I think that even with a simple invitation, it's good to capture a bit of the Burns magic – so I'd be tempted to add a quotation from a poem along the top or bottom as in the above example. You'll find other possible quotations in the Appendices (either in the poems or in the list of quotable phrases).

---

[36] *For our overseas friends – usually in a Scottish invitation you are bidden to come at 'X time for Y time' – X being the earliest you may arrive and Y the time all the guests are needed to be present.*

[37] *Again, for non UK readers, RSVP: Repondez S'il Vous Plait: Please reply.*

Version Two: The Garb of Auld Gaul

People can get awfully fussed about whether the invitation has to be written in Scots (or Lallans or the Doric or even the patois of a Glasgow pub). As with the invitation below, if you can carry it off with dignity and respect for the language and culture then go for it. (Mind you – you don't need to be too po-faced about it either!) If you feel uncomfortable – stick with the plain and simple.

Tae Jimmie an' Maggie

Frae Ann an' Clark

Ye are weel bidden tae oor

BURNS SUPPER

In oor hoose in Stinkin' Vennel, Dumfries
– onset hauf past seiven

On Setterday, Januar 25 2007

Let us ken if ye are comin'
Weir yer kilt

*'Oor Monarch's hinmost year but ane
Was five-an-twenty days began'*

Version Three: The Poetic Hijack

The third route would be to hijack, in the most reverent way possible, one of the party or invitational poems of the man himself. 'Here's a Bottle an' an Honest Friend'[38] or 'Whigham's Inn'[39] would lend themselves well to this. Or you could take and adapt some local song or traditional declamation from your town or region: the Common Riding for example, if you come from the Borders.

As long as you follow the underlying principle of a kind invitation, clearly expressed, you won't go wrong.

Dress – The kilt question (No, the other kilt question)

> *He set his Jenny on his knee,*
> *All in his Highland dress;*
> *For brawly weel he ken'd the way*
> *To please a bonnie lass!*[40]

As a guest receiving a beautiful invitation to a Burns Supper, one of your immediate concerns will be what to wear – especially (for once) if you are a man! Kilts attract a reasonable amount of controversy. Many agree with the horrified outburst of the German general in World War I: *'Hellfrauen'* – 'The Ladies From Hell'. And Generale Joffre is reported to have had (at least initially) the opinion: *'Pour l'amour, oui. Pour la guerre, non'.*[41]

The wearing of the kilt has grown a great deal in Scotland in the

---

[38] *This is used as the Epigraph at the beginning of this book.*
[39] *The words are the Epigraph at the end of this book.*
[40] *'Charlie is My Darling'.*
[41] *He changed his mind!*

last twenty years. It is now common to see grooms and ushers in kilts, young men at the rugby in kilts and rugby shirts, and, given an invitation to wear black tie, the dinner jacket[42] often yields to the Prince Charlie jacket or a Montrose doublet nowadays.[43]

The first point to make is that there is no law that obliges a Scot to wear the kilt to a Burns Supper. In fact, there is a level of irony in the whole tartan element seen at Burns Suppers as Burns was a lowlander. He would never have worn the kilt given its Highland nature and the fact that it was still illegal to wear the kilt in the aftermath of the Jacobite Rebellion from 1747[44] until

---

[42] *Or 'tuxedo' to our American friends.*

[43] *The 'Prince Charlie' is a short black jacket worn with a waistcoat and bow tie. The doublet is a closed, double-breasted coat worn with a jabot or lace frill at the throat.*

[44] *'An Act For The Abolition and Proscription of the Highland Dress 19 George II, Chap. 39, Sec. 17, 1746':*

'That from and after the first day of August, One thousand, seven hundred and forty-seven, no man or boy within that part of Britain called Scotland, other than such as shall be employed as Officers and Soldiers in His Majesty's Forces, shall, on any pretext whatever, wear or put on the clothes commonly called Highland Clothes (that is to say) the Plaid, Philabeg, or little Kilt, Trowse, Shoulder-belts, or any part whatever of what peculiarly belongs to the Highland Garb; and that no tartan or party-coloured plaid or stuff shall be used for Great Coats or upper coats, and if any such person shall presume after the said first day of August, to wear or put on the aforesaid garment or any part of them, every such person so offending, upon being convicted... shall suffer imprisonment without bail during the space of six months and no longer, and being convicted of a second offence... shall be liable to be transported to any of His Majesty's plantations beyond the seas, there to remain for the space of seven years.'

1782.[45] This is no place to go into the history of the kilt revival, but we can thank Sir Walter Scott for orchestrating the State Visit of HM King George IV to Scotland in 1822 and for persuading that fat and fashionable monarch to gird his ample loins in the Royal Stewart tartan.[46]

It is true that there is a Burns tartan (called 'the Burns Check') that is connected with the poet – to my mind more like an estate tweed than a true tartan[47] – but there is no compulsory link between the poet and the plaid.

---

[45] *'Repeal of the Act Prescribing the Wearing of Highland Dress 22 George III, Cap. 63, 1782.' The language of the Act is rather boring, but under its terms this proclamation was issued in Gaelic and English:*

'Listen Men. This is bringing before all the Sons of the Gael, the King and Parliament of Britain have forever abolished the act against the Highland Dress; which came down to the clans from the beginning of the world to the year 1746. This must bring great joy to every Highland Heart. You are no longer bound down to the unmanly dress of the Lowlander. *This is declaring to every Man, young and old, simple and gentle, that they may after this put on and wear the Truis, the Little Kilt, the Coat, and the Striped Hose, as also the Belted Plaid, without fear of the Law of the Realm or the spite of their enemies.' (Emphasis added.)*

[46] *Fortunately, the Prince Regent's decision to wear flesh-coloured tights did not become obligatory.*

[47] *A view shared by Ian Grimble in his* Scottish Clans and Tartans *(Hamlyn, 1973) whose opinion is that 'those fortunate enough to have inherited his name neither need pedigree nor clan history to enhance it. Certainly, the Burns Check would gild no lily.' (p33).*

That being said, the kilt is a wonderful sight (and is readily available for hire in many places, certainly in the UK, Australia/NZ, Canada and the USA) so why not have a go, gentlemen? There are a lot of views on the heraldic etiquette of the wearing of the tartan but this is how I interpret the 'rules':

- If you bear the name of a tartan-wearing clan, or your name is a sept (which is a branch) of one, then you and yours may wear that tartan. Many family tartans come in variations: 'Hunting' – which is a darker version; 'Ancient' – with muted colours; and 'Dress' – which has more white in it and is more often now worn by ladies. By extension you can wear your mother's (or your wife's) family tartan if you choose.

- If you have served in a Scottish Regiment or in a Pipe Band or Drum Corps (or Scout Troop) you may wear its colours.

- Similarly, hundreds of clubs and firms have registered tartans – milkmen in 'Robert Wiseman's Golden Jubilee' or brewers of The Caledonian Brewery; graduates of universities as far apart as Glasgow and Chicago; members and benefactors of charities including the Round Table and the National Trust. Rangers Football Club has an ordinary set and a dress set for ladies while members of the North West Mounted Police in Canada no doubt always get their woman while sporting their own tartan![48]

- There is a group of generic tartans which 'anyone' can wear – the Black Watch[49] (or Government Sett)[50] or the Royal Stewart (showing allegiance to HM the Queen).

---

[48] *I presume worn only in dismounted dress.*

[49] *Originally a non-clan tartan borne by the British army, by extension used for any in the service of HM Government which I guess includes UK taxpayers…*

[50] *Called a 'sett' or pattern rather than a tartan.*

Canada, the United States, Australia, New Zealand and each of the Canadian Provinces have their patterns too.

- There are even high fashion kilts nowadays – a 21st century take on our national dress where tartan is replaced by pinstripes, denim, jet black or even leather – albeit not for the faint hearted!

- The final category is: whatever the hire firm has in your size.

There are certainly enough designs to choose from, with official estimates of over 4,000 tartans in use, a number that is growing by over 100 every year. The recognition that tartan is one of the key attributes of Scotland led the Scottish Parliament to create The Scottish Register of Tartans to guard and guide this great tradition (and greater export) whose powers includes the rather unusual power to refuse to register a tartan if 'the name of the tartan is undesirable'.

There are many kiltmakers and hire firms with good websites which will answer your detailed questions about how to wear the kilt, and which accessories are needed. That really falls beyond the scope of today's book. However, as to the great and grave question – what do you wear below the kilt? – the answer is simple: *Socks and Shoes.*

We don't have time here to go through every item of kilt wear – but a couple of quick pointers for neophytes:

- **Sporrans** – 'what do you keep in them?' seems to be the most popular question. Just think of them as a single pocket and you'll have the right idea. There are many designs of sporran and so it is a chance to assert your personality.[51] The broad rule is that fluffy/hairy sporrans are for evening dress and plain leather are for daywear.

---

[51] *A good friend tells me that the boys at her son's school in Perthshire wear the kilt on Sundays and the boys suffer from 'sporran envy'... Size matters.*

- **Kilt Pins** – please *do not* use your kilt pin to close the two flaps of the kilt – it makes the garment hang badly and affects the circulation.[52]

- **Socks** – socks woven in the same tartan as your kilt, red and white 'diced' pattern, or pure cream[53] will complement your evening attire, while solid colours are best in the day. These are held in place by elastic garters with 'flashes' – little cloth tabs which are typically red or green (to match the predominant colour of your kilt).

- **Skean Dhu**[54] – the small knife carried traditionally in the right sock top (whether you are right handed or left handed).[55]

- **Shoes** – In strict full dress, ghillie brogues (with an open front and long, long laces you tie several times round your calf and ankles) or buckled black shoes are worn. In practice any shiny pair of black formal shoes will see you through the evening. In the day, brogues[56] (brown or black) are the benchmark, but are not mandatory nowadays.

---

[52] *Most kilt pins are small representations of broadswords or claymores, or family badges, or oddities like the foot of a grouse. If you are wearing an old fashioned pin – like a nappy/diaper pin – you should wear it with the clasp pointing downwards (correct form, albeit slightly counterintuitive).*

[53] *There is some controversy over whether white socks are permissible. Not my fight.*

[54] *Or Sgian Dhub, if you prefer. This is Gaelic for 'black knife' and is pronounced Skee-in Doo. This should not be confused with a 'dirk,' which is the larger, stabbing dagger worn (mainly by pipers) at the waist.*

[55] *Please remember that you can't take your Skean Dhu as hand baggage on a plane!*

[56] *Or 'wingtips' in American.*

[57] *And that's how much tartan material it takes to make a kilt. Maybe that's where the phrase comes from (with apologies to American footballers…).*

If you don't want to go the whole nine yards[57] for a formal occasion there are alternatives to the kilt. The trews[58] – or tartan trousers[59] can be worn with a mess coat or dinner jacket sometimes with a tartan waistcoat daringly cut on the bias (but *please* never a sporran with them) – or even just a tartan bow tie and/or cummerbund adds a festal touch to your standard evening dress and to the occasion.

Of course, this has assumed that the evening is 'full dress,' but

many Burns Suppers will be 'come as you are', where perhaps only the performers and the Top Table will be in evening dress, while the guests are in day wear – in this case, too, a touch of tartan looks good[60] and helps make you as a guest a part of the happening.

For the ladies? I am far too nervous to prescribe rules on party frocks for the fair even when tartan is really fashionable. At the risk of being howled down, this is a time where the male peacock struts about! The only advice I can give is – don't clash colours with your man's kilt and wear a complementary bit of tartan.

In general, ladies wear a black or white party dress, often with a

---

[58]   *There are some who hold strong views on the trews. In 1804, when the British Army debated abandoning the kilt in favour of the tartan trousers, the redoubtable Colonel Cameron (of the Cameron Highlanders, of course) petitioned the Prince Regent to retain the Highlandman's garb, opposing, as he called them, 'the whimsical tartan pantaloon'. As ever, the Camerons won the battle.*

[59]   *Military tailors assure me that there is a difference between trews (which have no outside seam) and trousers (which have). I don't think that would make much difference to good old Col Cameron.*

[60]   *Or a Burns Check tie.*

tartan sash over the shoulder. I believe that you should wear your sash pinned on your right shoulder (unless you are the wife of a chief,[61] when it is the left shoulder[62] – a privilege graciously extended to members of the Royal Scottish Country Dance Society by HM the Queen).

I recall seeing a set of complicated diagrams about how to tie your sash and where to pin your brooch, depending on whether you had adopted your husband's tartan or not. Too complicated for me – but I must look it up for the next edition.[63] In the meantime, though, I wouldn't take the preceding two paragraphs too seriously.

For non-formal dinners, ladies, come as you are – but again, a bit of tartan cheers up the process.[64]

---

[61] *If in doubt, check your husband's hatbox and see how many feathers he has – q.v. footnote 33.*

[62] *By analogy, the ladies of colonels of the Scottish Regiments have the same right.*

[63] *Broadly speaking, (a) women (married or unmarried) of a clan wear the sash over the right shoulder across the breast, secured by a pin or small brooch on the right shoulder (b) wives of chiefs and colonels wear a sash which may be fuller in size over the left shoulder and secured with a brooch on the left shoulder (c) ladies who have married out of their clans can use their original clan tartan in a longer sash worn over the right shoulder, secured there with a pin and fastened in a large bow on the left hip and (d) more rarely, country dancers or any lady needing to keep the front of the dress clear of the sash can use a small sash buttoned on at the back of the waist, or held by a small belt, with the sash secured at the right shoulder by a pin or small brooch so that the ends fall backwards from the right shoulder and swing at the back of the right. (Or anything more simple that comes to mind!)*

[64] *Maybe not lumberjack shirts, though... just like my dear papa.*

Whatever the dinner, the dress code or the weather – come dressed to have a great time.

Paraphernalia – Is there a Scots word for kitsch? [65]

Kirk-Alloway seemed in a bleeze,
Thro' ilka bore the beams were glancin',
And loud resounded mirth and dancin'.[66]

It's about half an hour before the start and you and your fellow guests are wending your way to the Supper. What will you find on the other side of the door when you arrive?

A great many Burns Suppers are relatively plain and look like any formal or semi-formal dinner, but an increasing number of organisers try to create more ambience. There are lots of ways of capturing a Scottish feel in the dining room without falling into a Bollywood remake of *Brigadoon* (Mind you, that might be rather memorable!):

- **Table cloths/napkins** (and if you are using paper plates, there are lots of possibilities for plates and cups) in tartan or tartan colours. White cloths with tartan runners and matching napkins are particularly good and relatively trouble free.

- **Place Mats** – again in tartan or with Scottish themes (perhaps shortbread tin scenes of majestic scenery, or less reverently, there are some on the market now with dic-

---

[65] *'Whigmaleeries' actually.*
[66] *'Tam o' Shanter'.*

tionary definitions of Scottish insults including 'Glaikit', 'Sumpf' and 'Ejit').[67]

- **Centrepieces** – heather, thistles[68] or flowers matching the tartan colours, with strong reds and greens and purples.

- **Flags and bunting** (a big flag outside your house will look pretty wonderful!)

    This is another area of potential confusion for visitors, as Scotland has two flags. The St Andrew's Cross (or Saltire) has a blue field with a white X shaped cross and is the National Flag of Scotland.[69]

    The Lion Rampant has a yellow field with a red lion

---

[67] *Pronounced: glay-kit – foolish or thoughtless; sumpf – a slow witted person; ee-jit – idiot.*

[68] *The Thistle is the national floral emblem of Scotland, commemorating the battle of Largs in 1263, when the Scots finally defeated the Norsemen under King Haakon IV of Norway, freeing the west of our country from the Vikings. Haakon's men, the better to effect a night attack, ran barefoot towards the sleeping Scots, only to tread on a bed of thistles. The cries of pain alerted the Scots, who put the Norwegians to flight. The highest honour in Scotland is still to be made a Knight of the Thistle (a personal gift of the Queen) whose motto, like the thistle, is 'Nemo Me Impune Lacessit,' variously translated as 'No one Touches Me With Impunity' or 'Wha Daur Meddle Wi' Me', or in Glasgow as 'You lookin' at me, Jimmie?' This motto was carried to the American colonies by Scots and can be seen on flags from the American War of Independence. It is still in traditional use in the US on wreaths and monuments to police officers who fall in the line of duty.*

[69] *The Saltire commemorates the victory of the Scots and Picts over the Saxons at Athelstaneford in 832 AD. Legend tells that St Andrew (the first apostle called by Jesus) gave the Scots the sign of victory by drawing his cross (he was crucified on an X shaped cross) in white clouds against the blue sky. (Must have been one of the few days it wasn't raining…).*

The Lion Rampant   **The Saltire**

raised on its back legs ready to fight, enclosed within a double red decorated border. This is the Royal Standard of Scotland and unless I am very lucky and you, dear Monarch, are reading this, readers should not technically use it.[70] That being said, both are widely available and used by all.

At home, candlelight and a flaming fire work well. If it's a sit down supper, have place cards with RB's head or a band of tartan or a thistle, with everyone's names handwritten on them.[71]

The Big Dinner organiser will work with the manager of the venue in creating what's feasible and within budget. Big corporate events tend to be more dramatic as there's a bigger budget – I've

---

[70] *Its use by other, non-authorised persons is an offence under the Act of Parliament 1672 cap. 47 and 30 & 31 Victoria cap. 17. (A warning from the Lord Lyon's website!) His Late Majesty King George V, by Royal Warrant of 3 September 1934 allows the use of the flag 'by loyal subjects' as a 'mark of loyalty'. This seems to indicate that wee flags on sticks (for waving at parades and possibly even on sandcastles) are OK, and bunting is probably alright, so you'll only get nicked if you fly the flag from a pole on top of your house. As Scotland is the last country in the world in which its chief herald (Lord Lyon) has a judicial court to try offenders – you have been warned (although, to be fair, the heralds are more liberal now than heretofore)!*

[71] *And maybe a short Burns quote relevant to each guest or as a theme for the evening.*

seen a former banking hall turned into a Scottish castle (complete with knights in armour); tables set in different tartans to match the hosts' kilts or set out like a lady's dancing outfit, crisp white table cloths with swags of tartan draped across like her sash.

When you are arranging your supper – a word of advice – whatever you choose, get the room(s) set up as early in the day as you can – it's going to be a busy few hours before your guests arrive!

Seating Plan and Tables

If it's a big dinner, the organisers will have a list of names and which table you should sit at (or a plan of the tables). This isn't the book to give you the low-down on how to set a formal seating plan – there are other books on the shelf for that. The Top Table probably needs a bit of explanation, however.

Larger dinners will have the speakers and their partners, possibly the organising committee and any local dignitaries or guests of honour on one table under the chairman of the event. The chairman has a hard role, being captain of the evening and therefore entirely responsible for the smooth flow of the festivities. There is some detailed advice later on for the 'lucky' incumbent, but as a general rule for those in the audience attending their first Supper, when you see the chairman stand up, then you are moving into the next phase of the evening and should stop and listen in silence.

Top Tables can be raised on a dais with the honoured folk along one side like a bench of judges; they can be on the floor in front of the band or even in the dead centre of the room. Typically the chairman will be in the middle, facing the largest part of the audience, with the Immortal Memory speaker to one side and either his/her spouse or the guest of honour on the other. The other speakers and entertainers are usually on the table, too, but

I have seen them spread through the room as well – which can be nice and inclusive.

When the chairman (or the venue manager) is ready, the Supper will be announced and guests should go to their tables – we are now nearly ready! Often, a formal Burns Supper will commence with a piper leading the chairman and Top Table guests to their place – the signal for festivities to begin![72]

---

[72] *At larger, more formal do's the Piper will lead in the Top Table, with the rest of the guests following at the back of the procession.*

The Burns Supper in Order

The Menu (or Bill o' Fare)

O sic a feast.[73]

So, the Top Table is in place, you've said 'hello' to the people beside you, and have a couple of moments to look over the menu. We will discuss the actual food soon – but what will the menu itself look like?

I like it when there's a thematic link between the invitation and the menu card. If the stationer has one, he'll have the other matching – either a single menu card (with the motif at the top) or a folded four-sider. You could do something pretty effective on the PC at home – how about a photo screened from last year? The St Andrew's Cross and the Stars and Stripes for a transatlantic do? Your clan badge? There are lots of colourful possibilities (please, of course, observe anyone's copyright).

The menu is quite important as it imparts important information about the food ahead and the structure of the evening. Both elements are vital in helping guests settle in and pace themselves.

The question I am most often asked is: 'should the menu be written in Broad Scots?' As this isn't one of McGinn's Three Precepts, I say anything goes.[74] On the plus side, it's part of our heritage and is characterful. To be fair to multicultural audiences, you should consider having a translation or description underneath the Scots. On the other hand, there is a relatively limited culinary language in Scots, so you sometimes see some neologisms.[75] One

---

[73]   *'The Twa Herds' – note that 'sic' is Scots for 'such' – not a reflection on the Haggis...*

[74]   *Or 'gae on yersel!'*

[75]   *A polite way to say the menu writer just makes up words to fit – not unlike menus in many trendy restaurants.*

thing is always perfectly permissible and that's to use the Scots phrase 'Bill o' Fare' instead of 'Menu'.

Before the list of food I like to see an appropriate Burns quotation (sometimes the grace is printed here so that people can follow the words if they haven't heard it before). Similarly at the end, if there is space, another passage could be added.

As well as the 'Bill o' Fare,' the menu card will list the speeches, speakers and entertainers. On a four pager, the chairman is usually on the front, but could be at the top of the speaker's list instead. If whoever is writing the menu knows Burns well and has a good sense of humour, you will often find a short Burns quote relevant to each of the speakers, perhaps with a gentle joke at the expense of someone's job or personal characteristic.

If there is a fourth page the organiser can help the troops by printing the words of 'Auld Lang Syne' or any other songs that the singers want to open up to the company. A good idea if there is to be proper dancing afterwards is to have the programme of dances as agreed with the band to help people plan their setts.

Here is a rough template:

The Heidrum-Hodrum Golf Club
125th Annual Burns Supper

Jock Tamson
Club Captain and Chairman

Weedram Hall
25 January 2009

Front (of four)

Bill o' Fare

Some hae meat and canna eat
And some wad eat that want it
But we hae meat and we can eat
An sae the Lord be thankit

Grace   *Rev. I M Jolly*

Loch Fyne Smoked Salmon
Chablis, 1998

●

THE HAGGIS
Wi' Champit Tatties an' Bashit Neeps

Piped in with Honours by Master Thomas Thom
Addressed by Miss Lizzie Borden

Laphroig, 10 y/o

●

Contrefilet of Aberdeen Angus Beef

With Sauté Potatoes and Seasonal Vegetables

Claret, 1994

●

Scots Trifle

Cheese and Biscuits

Coffee and Liqueurs

'We arena' fu, we've just had plenty'
There will be a fifteen minute interval before the speeches

Inside Left (of four) or
Front (of two)

Speeches An' Ploys

The Queen

The Chairman

'Among the illustrious Scottish sons'

The Immortal Memory

Major General Sir Richard Hannay KCB, DSO
'Why the deuce should I repine, An' be an ill-forboder?
I'm 23 and five foot nine, I'll go an' be a sodger'

•

Tam o' Shanter

Recited by Glen Morangie

•

The Lassies

The Rev. John Knox
'Here am I, a chosen sample,
To show Thy grace is great and ample'

The Reply

Mary Stewart, Countess of Bothwell
'True it is she has ae failing,
Had ae woman ever less?'

•

Burns Songs   *Bob Maxwell, Fiddler*
Pipe Medley   *Pipe Major Buster Eardrums*

Auld Lang Syne

The Company

Inside Right (of four) or
Back (of two)

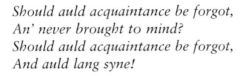

Should auld acquaintance be forgot,
An' never brought to mind?
Should auld acquaintance be forgot,
And auld lang syne!

For auld lang syne, my dear,
For auld lang syne.
We'll tak a cup o' kindness yet,
For auld lang syne.

An' there's a hand, my trusty fiere!
An' gie's a hand o' thine!
An' we'll tak a right gude willie waught,
For auld lang syne.

For auld lang syne, my dear,
For auld lang syne.
We'll tak a cup o' kindness yet,
For auld lang syne.

Back (of four)

The Grace

He wales a portion with judicious care;
And 'Let us worship God!' he says with solemn air.[76]

In the middle of your perusal of the Bill o' Fare, or your chat with the nice person beside you, or your growing intimacy with the bottle of malt on the table, the chairman will rise and welcome one and all to the Burns Supper. Sometimes this includes a short[77] introduction to what's ahead.

In every case, the chairman will call for a moment's silence for grace to be pronounced. It's a fine thing to stop and think for a moment, as we stand in our party clothes with more food than many will have in a week and give thanks.

Sometimes, a minister is approached to perform this (minister of religion, as I wouldn't think that government ministers by and large are any closer to Heaven than the rest of us), or else any member of the company with particular gravitas. This failing, like everything else on the night, if there's no-one to do it, it's the chairman's job. Grace is said either just before everyone sits down (in which case the chairman calls for silence and the guests all stand behind their chairs, heads bowed until joining in the 'Amen' if so moved) or just before the service of the first course of dinner, when people are in their seats (everyone remains sitting, heads bowed as before).

Nine times out of ten, the grace pronounced over the company will be the Selkirk Grace, which appears in various forms and spellings, but most often this one:

---

[76] *'The Cottar's Saturday Night'.*

[77] *And I mean short – if you are the chairman please remember we have a lot to do together tonight!*

Some hae meat and canna eat
And some wad eat that want it
But we hae meat and we can eat
An sae the Lord be thankit.[78]

The origination of this prayer is one of the ten events in the Burnsian Critical Decathlon (the other nine will feature elsewhere). At the simplest level, Burns is recorded as saying grace in these words at the table of the Earl of Selkirk in July 1793. There was a version of this grace current though, called either the 'Covenanter's Grace', the 'Kirkcudbright[79] Grace' or the 'Galloway Grace' but it was Burns who captured and crystallised what we say today.[80]

Whatever the controversy, the verse is now as firmly embedded in the religious culture of Scotland as 'Amazing Grace'. There are some Burnsians who object to the presence of religion at the Supper given Rabbie's well-known stroppy relationship with organised religion. My personal view is that RB fought with the Kirk, not the Lord, and that even a relatively irreligious educated man of the eighteenth century was probably more of a believer than the majority of people in Britain today.

It's not Burns's only attempt at the genre. There are a number of less reverential approaches with the poet's tongue firmly in his cheek:

O Lord, when hunger pinches sore,
Do thou stand us in stead,
An' send us, from thy bounteous store,
A tup or wether head! Amen.[81]

---

[78] *'Amen' can be (and usually is) added at the end.*

[79] *For non-Scots – pronounced 'Kir-Koobray.'*

[80] *The Selkirk Arms Hotel in Kirkcudbright has a plaque on its wall claiming that Burns wrote the grace there.*

[81] *A tup is a young ram, and a wether is a two year old ram. There is another difference, but as we are in mixed company, we'd better draw a blank over it. Sheep's head was a common dish until relatively recently.*

> *O Lord, since we have feasted thus,*
> *Which we so little merit,*
> *Let Meg now take away the flesh,*
> *An' Jock bring in the spirit! Amen.*[82]

Or some genuinely touching prayers like this one:

> *O Thou who kindly dost provide*
> *For every creature's want!*
> *We bless Thee, God of Nature wide,*
> *For all Thy goodness lent:*
> *An' if it please Thee, Heavenly Guide,*
> *May never worse be sent;*
> *But, whether granted, or denied,*
> *Lord, bless us with content. Amen!*[83]

At larger dinners organised by clubs or institutions, sometimes the grace particular to the group is used instead of a Burns composition.

Once upon a time a grace after dinner was common too – but not today – and you will find some good examples in RB's smaller verses. Even at the smaller Home Suppers this is a kind tradition to follow and the sentiment and words of the Selkirk Grace are pretty inclusive theologically of all conditions and manners of men.

If you don't say grace habitually at your family dinner table, have a practice before the Supper to avoid any misunderstanding,

---

such as what happened to one family not so many years ago. Mum and Dad were having the minister and his wife to dine. As a treat their son was allowed to sit at table. The Reverend Gentleman (a 'teeth-will-be-provided' preacher) glowered as the food arrived on the table without prayer. 'Will wee Jamie say Grace?' he inquired. The child looked slightly blank until his mother prompted him – 'You know; remember what your Dad said before supper last night'. She tried to help further, 'He started with "O God!".' Wee James remembered, and solemnly intoned:

'O God! Not the minster and his boring wife for dinner again!' Here endeth the Lesson.

Food

> *On thee aft Scotland chows her cood,*
> *In souple scones, the wale o' food!*
> > *Wi' kail an' beef;*
> *But when thou pours thy strong heart's blood,*
> > *There thou shines chief.*
>
> *Food fills the wame, an' keeps us leevin';*
> *Tho' life's a gift no worth receivin',*
> *When heavy-dragg'd wi' pain an' grievin';*
> > *But, oil'd by thee,*
> *The wheels o' life gae down-hill, scrievin',*
> > *Wi' rattlin' glee.*[84]

So the food is about to come out of the kitchen – what should you expect?

One of the joys of being a guest at a good Burns Supper is the savouring of Scotland's fine native produce – both food and drink. Many folk find it easy to believe in the latter, but get a bit

---

[84] *'Scotch Drink.'*

nervous of the former given the bad press received by Scottish cookery, possibly as some of the traditional names seem a bit too esoteric to see on the Ready Meal counter at Marks & Spencer:

Crappit Heids	Fat Brose
Stoorum	Partan Bree
Inky-Pinky	Clap Scones
Nackit	Snoddie
Fitless Cock	Whim-wham
Rumbledethumps	Whaupmaheid[85]

And some of you were worried about the haggis?

If you are arranging a large Supper then no doubt the caterer will help you choose a good meal within your budget, avoiding the perils of the rubber chicken dinner. Have a look through this chapter for some ideas, while we address our home cooks and in so doing, give a flavour of traditional Scots cookery to anyone with lingering nerves about what's going to be on the plate in front of them next Friday.

As this is but a brief manual, there's little time to go through all the possibilities. For a more extensive list, please read some of the excellent cookery books available. I have presented here just enough ideas to get you started.

Soup and Starters

What can you expect for your first course?

I am torn on this one. When a 'cauld, cauld Januar' wind' is blowing there's nothing like a good hot plate of soup to take the chill off the guests and add some warmth to the company. So let's look at soup first.

---

[85]   OK – *I made that one up, but the others are all-too-real!*

My respectful suggestion is that there are three possibilities: Scotch Broth, Cock-a-leekie or Cullen Skink. As Scotch Broth is the only aspect of Scotland which impressed Dr Samuel Johnson, it probably deserves pride of place.[86]

	Pros	Cons
Scotch Broth	• Very traditional • Cheap • Nourishing (i.e. the barley helps to soak up the alcohol)	• If you're not a barley fan it's a bit off-putting • Needs to hang around the kitchen for three days to reach maturity
Cock-a-leekie	• Recipe is simple: Mrs Baxter's tin plus a tin opener • Can add prunes to the chickens and leeks to be ultra traditional and start a foodie argument	• Silly name – open to double entendres
Cullen Skink	• A thick and warm chowder which adds a nice colour to the menu • Fish soup – so suitable for most Veggies	• The name can be off-putting • Not as good for large dinners as it cools quickly

[86] *'Do you like our Scots broth, Dr Johnson?' 'Ah, very good for hogs, I believe.' 'Then let me help you to a little more.' To be fair to the Great Cham, when asked by Boswell 'You never ate it before?' Samuel replied 'No Sir, but I do not care how soon I shall eat it again.' James Boswell, 'The Journal of a Tour to the Hebrides,' Folio Society, London 1990, p178.*

On the starters side the traditional options would be fishy or meaty.

Scotland's fish produce is wonderful. A very simple plate of fine smoked salmon or shellfish is ideal and looks pretty on the plate. A bit more adventurous would be herring – the 'silver darlings' of Scotland: either sweet marinated fillets, or cooked in oatmeal – which is well worth the effort. If you are cooking and don't have a good fishmonger near you, there are some wonderful artisan companies on the net who can deliver by post.

If you are a meat eater and need a fix of something red this early in the show, game is a good bet. How about a pâté (possibly with redcurrant sauce or chutney – note that Cumberland sauce would be an injudicious choice at this event)[87] or a slice of game pie? Both are easy ways to access Scotland's long tradition of eating wee birdies and furry animals.

Don't forget that there's a long night ahead so you need to balance the portions well, not too much, not too little. We want everyone at the table to have some room left for the haggis!

The 'Address to a Haggis'

> *Ye Pow'rs wha gie us a' that's gude,*
> *Still bless auld Caledonia's brood,*
> *With great John Barleycorn's heart's blude,*
> *   In stowps or luggies,*
> *And on our board, the king of food,*
> *   A glorious Haggis!*[88]

---

[87] *Despite having Handel write 'Hail, the Conqu'ring Hero Comes' for him, the Duke of Cumberland, remains best known to history as 'Butcher Cumberland' because of his single-minded savagery after the battle of Culloden in 1746.*

[88] *This is the first version of the last stanza of the great Address To The Haggis, as originally published in* The Caledonian Mercury, *December 1786.*

Of the many worries and queries attending the Burns Supper, the haggis is first to rear its ugly head (for the more gullible reader: the head is so ugly, it's cut off before serving, which is why the haggis looks more like a sausage than a beastie). The humble haggis gets more bad press than any other food – unfairly.[89]

The questions are threefold: What's in it? What do you mean by 'Addressing' it? Do I have to eat it?

Beyond the traditional delight of being asked how one hunts the haggis by an American tourist (silly question – don't they know it was the first thing banned when New Labour came to power?) there is a great mythology about the haggis. For our purposes, I have neither the time nor the strength to weigh the arguments in favour of its French birth, or its being some dinosaur of Imperial Roman cooking.[90] The great secret I want to reveal to the public is this: haggis is delicious![91]

There is an old saying in politics: there are two things the public should not see: the making of laws and the making of sausages. And that applies to haggis *par excellence*. I wouldn't even begin to cook my own haggis from scratch and so at home we buy

89 *Even in* The Simpsons: '*Get yer haggis right here! Chopped heart and lungs, boiled in a wee sheep's stomach! Tastes as good as it sounds!' Willie the Scottish janitor, in 'Lisa the Beauty Queen.'*

90 *Read the relevant chapters of the classic Scottish culinary book, F Marian McNeill,* The Scots Kitchen, *Edinburgh 1929.*

91 *Sir Chris Hoy Scotland's most successful Olympic gold medallist swears by a training diet of haggis and Red Bull. Seems to work.*

from the wonderful Macsween's (as always, there is a strong counter opinion in favour of Hall's of Broxburn – who do have one of the best delivery van number plates: HAG 1S).[92] Of course, there are many local butchers in communities all over Scotland who make fine produce for their local market, too.

Both Macsween's and Hall's will ship haggis across the globe, bringing the Taste of Scotland closer to all. The biggest exception is the US, where the importation of fresh meat product (particularly sheep's lungs, for some reason or other) is strictly prohibited by the authorities. In a more carefree world ten or more years ago I did hear of the odd smuggler (I always imagined long haggises, one down each trouser leg, a bit like in *The Great Escape*...). There was a wheeze to have it shipped as animal feedstuff and then reintegrated to its paunch, but this may have been apocryphal.

There are a number of specialist butchers who have mastered the haggis State-side, but we always used Mr Lamb, whose company, Lamb Etc., is based in Oregon. He is a haggis aficionado (and a genealogy buff, too, so expect to have your family tree opened up while you arrange your haggis) and his produce is wonderful stuff which can be shipped all across the continental States.[93]

There are similar restrictions in Canada, Australia, New Zealand, Japan, China and the Republic of Ireland. The Swiss, for some bizarre reason, allow shipment, but only up to 2kg maximum (which is a reasonable amount of Toblerone, but little enough haggis for a party).

---

[92]   *Reportedly purchased for the princely sum of £18,000, which equates to a lot of haggises. And, before you ask, no-one is certain of the plural of haggis – so if you need two, go to the butcher, ask for one haggis and then say 'I'll just have another while you're there.'*

[93]   *There are purveyors of tinned haggis who can ship abroad – but I just can't see the Addressor indicting: 'His tin-opener, wi' ready slight.'*

If you are getting your haggis shipped, please make sure that you are home on delivery day. When we lived in Scarsdale, New York, DHL left a card explaining that they had attempted to deliver a package from Lamb Etc., but as it contained 'dangerous chemical and/or hazardous materials' they couldn't leave it on the doorstep.

If you have to cook your own, or are just interested in the recipe (like those little boys who have to stick a pole in a pond to see what's at the bottom) here goes. Those of you who are happy in ignorance should skip the next page. Be warned, however, that PG Wodehouse was convinced that the true recipe for haggis could be found in Shakespeare – *Macbeth*, Act 4, SC 1, l 14.[94]

My own view is simpler – McGinn's Three Step Recipe for the Haggis:

1   **BUY** a sheep.
2   **SELL** the wool.
3   **COOK** the rest.

This (more orthodox) recipe is for those who insist on more[95] detail.

Ingredients

The stomach bag of a sheep, the sheep's offal (including heart, lungs or 'lights', and liver), beef-suet, coarse pin-head oatmeal, onions, plenty of black pepper, salt and cayenne pepper.

Toast until brown a large cupful of oatmeal in the oven (or before the kitchen fire if you have one). Clean the large stomach bag thoroughly, firstly using copious cold water to wash it clean (keep changing the water and repeat as often as needed until the water stays reasonably

---

94   *'Eye of newt, and toe of frog'* etc.
95   *Grisly.*

clear and there is little sediment left) then, after turning it inside out and scalding it with fresh boiled water, scrape with a blunt knife. Then let it soak overnight in a pan of cold salty water.[96]

Next day get it out of the pan and lay it to one side, turning the shaggy side outermost. Drain the heart and liver (often called the pluck) of their blood, washing them thoroughly, and put on the boil, along with the lungs, completely covered with fresh cold water. It is important to have the windpipe hanging over the side of the pot to allow any vestigial impurities to drain.[97] After boiling for ninety minutes, cut away the tubes and pipes and any excessive[98] gristle. Take the heart and lights and mince them quite fine, then grate about half the liver. Take the minced pluck and the grated liver and mix them in a large bowl with half a pound of minced suet and two fine chopped medium onions of a strong flavour, then add the toasted oatmeal. Season the mixture with an appropriate amount of black pepper and rough salt, adding the final flourish of a healthy pinch of cayenne pepper. As soon as the liquid in which the pluck was boiled cools to room temperature, add as much of it as will cover the mixture until you reach what is often described as a 'sappy'[99] texture.

Once you have the correct consistency, take the stomach and fill the bag a bit over half full, to allow sufficient room for expansion. Press the mixture down firmly to expel any

---

[96] *This gives you time to change your mind and buy one.*

[97] *Please ensure that you place a small bowl under the windpipe to catch the dripping fluids.*

[98] *I can't think what might constitute non-excessive gristle.*

[99] *A Scottish word whose dictionary definition is 'moist, juicy or unctuous.'*

air then, with a stout needle and heavy thread, sew the bag up neatly and securely and place into another pot of fresh, boiling water with half a pint of lamb stock added (some recipes call for the substitution of half a pint of milk). Keep a close watch on its boiling – the moment you see it swell, prick it all over with a large bodkin to prevent its bursting. Boil the haggis on a rolling boil without the lid for three hours, topping up with boiling water as needed to keep the haggis covered.

Serve your homemade haggis very hot with the traditional trimmings.

Or if you have wisely acquired a haggis from your favourite butcher – you just need to re-heat it. I find the best way is to take the haggis out of any external plastic case and wrap it firmly in aluminium foil. Place the package in a large pot of boiling water and simmer gently for about 40 minutes for each pound (450g).[100]

One thing that everyone knows about a Burns Supper is that the Haggis gets Addressed. As we've finished our starters, now's the time!

There is a lot of mystery and controversy about how to Address the Haggis. The essentials of the ritual are commonly agreed by all factions: this is when a very large haggis has one of Burns's best-loved poems, 'Address To A Haggis', recited over it before being served for dinner to the assembled company.

So how do we do it?

At the front of the dining room stands a table (or the Top Table) where the Addressor will perform. On that table we need three glasses (or quaichs)[101] for the Addressor, the Chef and the Piper,

---

[100] *It's also very easy and effective to microwave a haggis (again removing it from its casing to avoid catastrophic explosions).*

[101] *A small shallow drinking cup with two handles – from the Gaelic for cup;* cuach *– now often in pewter or silver.*

and a carving knife as large as can be found in the kitchen. I like to use something that would have made Blackbeard blush, but any sharp instrument will suffice. (Using your own Skean Dhu is not advisable, as it takes ages to get the wee bits of haggis out of your kilt sock.)

To the sound of the pipes[102] (a rousing march[103] – see the whole discussion about Pipe Music below) the procession of Piper and Chef comes into the room – the chef carries the haggis[104] on a platter[105] festooned with green herbs or parsley and maybe tartan ribbons[106] and they walk around the room, circulating through the tables so that the punters get a good look at the next course while clapping in time to the music. Sometimes, the rear is brought up by a bearer carrying the whisky for the toast – either a couple of bottles, or a decanter and glasses on a tray. Quite

memorably, the St Andrew's Society of the State of New York adds two big guys with two big claymores as an honour guard.

The audience, hopefully with a wee (or large) dram inside, will clap in time with the music.[107] The audience might be invited by the chair-

---

[102] *Except in one of the oldest of clubs, our buddies in Paisley, who have a fiddler, not a piper.*

[103] *There is no firm rule about using a particular tune, but many pipers like to use Burns's 'A Man's A Man For A' That', which is a pretty good sentiment for the evening.*

[104] *Increasingly in the US all of the haggises needed to feed the company are brought out, but that's not strictly necessary.*

[105] *Not, please, on a china plate – as happened in New York once – the plate ended up in more bits than the haggis…*

[106] *I have even seen it decorated with stag's antlers – looking like a very devilish sausage indeed.*

[107] *Or at least clap…*

man to stand at this point, though I prefer to have everyone sitting down so that all the audience can see what's going on.

The Chef deposits the haggis in front of the Addressor and the Chef and Piper flank him,[108] standing at a safe distance to avoid collateral damage.

I'll talk about the Address in a moment, but once the deed is done, the Addressor gives his two colleagues their drams[109] and the three of them lead the company in toasting the haggis – with a flourish. The Chef recovers the last mortal remains of the beast (sometimes with the big knife still stuck in) and to the 'Black Bear' or some other valedictory march, the Piper leads him out by a slightly more direct route to the kitchen.

So, what can we expect of the Address itself?

As in everything, there are at least two schools of thought and practice: this time they are the Poetic and the Dramatic.

Many people are embarrassed at the thought of being seen in public talking to a large sausage. The Poetic Addressor (or PA) only sees the beauty of the rolling words of Burns. The rhythm of the stanzas is the keynote here – a simple approach which gives good results, particularly if people (roughly) understand the text. If you aren't quite sure yourself – have a look at Appendix 1 where I've had a stab[110] at translating the poem.

---

[108] *Along with any members of the Honour/Honor Guard.*

[109] *Quite often you will see the chairman or the addressor give the piper and chef their drams before the Address starts – usually with a toast between them: 'Weel played, piper!' from the chairman, and the traditional Gaelic toast 'Slainte mhath' (pronounced 'Slan-jay vah' and meaning 'Good health') in reply. You will regularly hear 'Slainte mhath' from a toaster and the reply 'Slainte mhor' ('Slan-jay vour' or 'Great health') from the toastee.*

[110] *Pun intended...*

The only 'business' in the PA approach is that the Addressor needs to take the knife at the line beginning 'His knife', wipe it on his/her sleeve ('dicht'), then cut the haggis at the words 'an' cut ye up'. The incomparable F Marian McNeill advises cutting with the point of the knife in the shape of a St Andrew's cross, the better to avoid explosion. In any case, the Addressor should check how thick the casing is – my very first Address (at Ayr Academy) involved attacking a locally produced haggis encased in industrial grade polythene – the knife bounced back and nearly took the Rector's hand off...

There is a growing and honourable tradition which allows the Addressor a few moments to reflect on the ceremony, with a joke or an anecdote, before setting forth on the recitation. I rather like this as it can add an extra element of comprehension (and a good laugh) to the proceedings. These comments though should be short and punchy (and don't forget the wrath that will fall upon your head – worse than the fate granted to a hundred haggises – if you steal one of the jokes from the later speakers).

After the poem is recited, the Addressor invites the whole company to toast 'The Haggis' before it is carried out to the kitchen.

The other approach is the Dramatic Address (or DA). The DA is the ultimate show off (in the nicest possible way). Legend has it that RB wrote the Address as a *jeu d'esprit* extempore at the house of a Mauchline friend (John Morrison, a cabinet maker) whose wife served haggis for dinner, and was apologetic for serving up a poor man's dinner to the Bard. Certainly it has a mirth and humour about it that allows the Addressor to go for some good laughs from the audience.[111]

---

[111] *Some say it was written for Adam Bruce who lived at Castlehill in Edinburgh (where Luath's offices are today) and others believe some Kilmarnock lawyers had it composed for their Haggis Club. I think it's more of the country than the town.*

At its simplest level, the DA brings actions into the address to provide both entertainment and elucidation. It's not a great idea to try and express this in words, but the publishers vetoed a DVD to accompany the book on the grounds of cost (who said that Scots weren't mean?). So here's a few of the ideas.

Text	Action
Fair fa' your honest, sonsie face, Great chieftain o' the puddin-race!	Look adoringly at the haggis – treat it like a pretty girl's face (I didn't say this would be easy!)
Aboon them a' ye tak your place, Painch, tripe, or thairm:	Count to three on your fingers.
Weel are ye wordy of a grace As lang's my arm.	Show how long your arm is.
The groaning trencher there ye fill,	Lift the haggis platter as if it were a ton weight.
Your hurdies like a distant hill, Your pin wad help to mend a mill In time o' need	Pat your bottom.
While thro' your pores the dews distil Like amber bead.	Point to the haggis (or if brave enough run a finger along it).
His knife see rustic Labour dight,	Take the knife and polish it on your arm (carefully, please).
An' cut ye up wi' ready slight, Trenching your gushing entrails bright, Like onie ditch;	Cut the haggis.
And then, O what a glorious sight, Warm-reeking, rich!	Drop the knife and open your arms towards the haggis in admiration.
Then horn for horn, they stretch an' strive:	Make scooping movements with both hands; rub your fat tummy.
Deil tak the hindmost, on they drive, Till a' their weel-swall'd kytes belyve	

Text	Action
Are bent like drums;	
Then auld Guidman, maist like to rive, 'Bethankit!' hums.	Make a belchy/farty joke.[112]
Is there that owre his French ragout,	Act scornfully over the foreign foods.
Or olio that wad staw a sow, Or fricassee wad mak her spew Wi' perfect scunner, Looks down wi' sneering, scornfu' view On sic a dinner?	
Poor devil! see him owre his trash, As feckless as a wither'd rash, His spindle shank a guid whip-lash, His nieve a nit;	Point to a member of the audience (or the Chef if he's agreeable), hold a finger up for 'rash' (a reed) and make a little nut with your fingers for 'nit' (a nut).
Tho' bluidy flood or field to dash, O how unfit!	Make a dismissive gesture.
But mark the Rustic, haggis-fed,	Point to another audience member (maybe the Piper?)
The trembling earth resounds his tread,	Make big stamping noise.
Clap in his walie nieve a blade, He'll make it whistle;	Pick up the knife.
An' legs, an' arms, an' heads will sned Like taps o' thrissle.	Slash it round about your head a few times (watch out for haggis crumbs...).
Ye pow'rs, wha mak mankind your care, And dish them out their bill o' fare, Auld Scotland wants nae skinkin' ware, That jaups in luggies;	Hold up your hands in invocation.

---

[112] 'Pardon...'

Text	Action
But if ye wish her gratfu' prayer, Gie her a Haggis!	Pick up the haggis.[113] After the deafening applause, raise your glass and invite the whole audience to stand and toast 'The Haggis' before it is borne off kitchen-wards.

The real joy in the DA, though, are the twiddles and nuances that each interpreter builds up over the years. The great DA performers, like the great PAS, use their own experiences to give a personal insight into the works of Burns.[114]

The most exotic specimen of the DA is the Turbo Charged Address – there are a few supremely gifted Haggis Murderers including Group Captain the Rev. Donald Wallace who has had the freehold of the Address Platform at the Scottish Bankers' Burns Supper for over thirty years. His erudite and entertaining introduction keep the attention of a famously difficult audience, while his rendition of the Address itself is given with the vigour of a storm and is capped by the wonderful *coup de théâtre* when at the words 'an' legs and arms and heids will sned' he chops off the tops of the five candles in the candelabrum beside him. (The redoubtable Walter MacGregor on the other hand, knocks off the chef's high hat or toque at the same point. I presume that Cheffie is allowed his whisky in advance to steady his nerves, particularly if Walter has had one or two to steady his hand!)

There is also the sing-a-long approach (like *The Rocky Horror Show* or *The Sound of Music*) where the audience participates with gestures, props and calls. This is no bad thing. I can see a

---

[113] *On the tray, of course!*

[114] *Remember, please, that these are but suggestions to guide the wise, not rules for fools to follow – try out your own style and interpretation!*

whole audience primed to contribute noises and actions: a groan at 'groaning trencher'; a wiggle for 'hurdies'; waving a knife at 'his knife'; a Bisto Kids sniff at 'warm-reeking'; a 'yuk' at 'sic a dinner'; a 'Boo!' at 'poor devil'; a resounding cheer at 'Rustic'; stamping of feet under the table at 'trembling earth'; waving the main course knife again at 'legs an' arms'; culminating in a heart-felt 'gie her a Haggis' with the company cheering in unison.

Maybe a tad rich – but I wouldn't mind trying it one day!

What is the point of the Address? I would respectfully suggest that it's the premedication before the main operation, to ease the patient (though most of the audiences I know have been impatient) before the surgeon comes. A good address, DA or PA, builds a community around the Addressor and the ceremony – doing this well builds a platform for success as the evening moves on.

The Haggis Course

So, having now explained the ceremony and importance of the haggis, let's look at its most honoured place in the feast. It is rare nowadays to have haggis as the main course of the dinner – it is normally served as an intermediate course (analogous with a fish course). If upon trying it you don't care for the taste, no-one will be offended (but do, please, try it at least). Don't forget also that there are different approaches to making a haggis – one where the oats predominate and a darker version with more liver while some butchers use pork rather than lamb or a mixture of meats and even game. Try both the light and the dark varieties if you can and compare – you may prefer one, or you may happily feast on both.

At a formal dinner, after the Addressed Haggis is carried off, pre-arranged plates of haggis and its traditional accompaniments ('champit tatties' – mashed potatoes – and 'bashit neeps' – mashed turnip) are placed before each diner. So as not to waste the celebratory haggis there should perhaps be a tradition that the Addressor,

Piper and Chef have to eat the whole lot to preserve it from dishonour – but that's maybe a bit keen. Often an extra bowl will be brought out for those who are up for second helpings.

At a sit down at home, I'd recommend the Addressor serves the haggis, while the guests help themselves to neeps and tatties from pots placed on the table.

Now, to dangerous territory – what is a neep? This is one of the most frequent questions from people in the audience and, believe it or not, it's a tricky one to answer.

In travelling the world (even in travelling the UK) speaking about

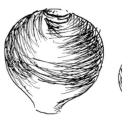

Burns, I have had more problems with this root vegetable that anything else. Due to a combination of history, mistranslation and human folly, no one in the world can agree which vegetable is which. Fortunately this is one of the few human controversies that hasn't broken out into internecine war, so let's keep our fingers crossed that wiser counsel will continue to prevail.

When I first came to London (and wrestled with the butchers over the absence of Lorne sausage[115] and Gigot chops), many's the time I enjoyed philosophical arguments with local greengrocers over what I wanted and what they were going to sell me in the turnip line. I soon discovered that there is an invisible line across Great Britain where the nomenclature of *brassicae* commits a *volte face*. So to forestall any future crises: here's my quick guide to the Neep Minefield:

---

[115] *This square sausage is named after music hall legend Tommy Lorne whose catchphrase was 'sausages are the boys!' There's even a campaign to make it a protected food brand like Parma Ham!*

Interest Group	Vegetable description	
	Larger Purple tinge Orange Flesh	Small Greenish tinge Pale/White Flesh
Scientists	*Brassica napobrassica*	*Brassica rapa*
Scots	Turnip or Neep (or Tumshie)	Swede
England north of the magic divide	Turnip	Swede
Southern England	Swede	Turnip
America	Rutabaga (or Yellow Turnip)	Turnip (or White Turnip)
Sweden	Rotabagga	Unknown

Neeps, of course, have another purpose in Scottish culture – making jack o' lanterns at Halloween – it was a joy when we moved to the US to be able to use nice soft pumpkins rather than suffering the agonising work of hollowing out a neep!

The neep has a close link to Burns as it was introduced into Scotland by Patrick Miller of Dalswinton, who was given rutabaga seeds by King Gustav III of Sweden. As it was Miller who leased Ellisland to Burns, RB may have been one of the first farmers to sow the crop. Certainly, I hope Miller introduced them when he attended his first Burns Supper.

Cooking them is child's play (it is the dicing that hurts!) – boil in salted water for about twenty minutes until tender, add some butter and mash to a rough consistency. In some families a small pinch of mace is added at the end,[116] but I have no great opinion on this one way or the other.

---

[116]   *F Marian McNeill quotes an old recipe: 'mashed turnips … are considerably improved by the … seasoning of ginger, which, besides, corrects the flatulent properties of this esculent' (Scots Kitchen, p129).*

SECTION TWO: THE BURNS SUPPER   81

As for the potatoes – get any nice large potato that mashes well, boil it and mash it! The potatoes should be of a smoother puree than the turnips (hence the use of differing adjectives in the Scots phrase: '*champit* tatties and *bashit* neeps').

You can get a tad more elaborate and look to a mix of potatoes and turnips (such as clapshot from Orkney – equal quantities of boiled potatoes and boiled turnips mashed together with a bit of butter or dripping and salt and pepper to taste – sometimes sprinkled with chopped chives) but I prefer the mix of colours; the dark, grainy haggis balanced by the orange, slightly lumpy turnips and the smooth creamy white of the tatties.

What to drink? I'll give you three guesses!

I like to tell any 'haggis virgins' in the company that there is a glass of good malt beside the plate, and you can use it in one of two ways: aesthetically, by pouring it over the haggis, or anaesthetically, by pouring it down your throat. In truth, I prefer my haggis without 'gravy' and usually serve it with a nice claret[117] or an interesting Australian red. My Wife-and-Dancing-Partner doesn't drink red wine (she's allergic to tannin and so won't chew shoe leather either) so, after a number of experiments, she tends to use a mid-priced New Zealand sauvignon blanc.

People can get awfully fussed about the haggis and its composition – but I defy anyone on a cold wintry night to tuck into haggis, neeps and tatties and not come out the other end a happier person!

(And the leftover haggis is wonderful reheated for breakfast.)

The Main Course

For centuries, outsiders saw the Scots as a poor nation and poorer cooks. Over the last few decades, the quality of restaurant dining in

---

[117] *As red Bordeaux wine is known in Britain.*

our country has improved and you can now buy Scottish cookbooks in most bookshops.

This means that the organiser of the larger, catered Burns Supper can work with the Chef to choose something effective and enjoyable as the culinary keystone of the evening. If you are choosing the menu please do take care not to be too elaborate. When perusing the Bill o' Fare you are likely to find some of the high-quality produce of Scotland.

- **Salmon** – best of all, wild – grilled or roasted and served with a little light hollandaise.
- **A Gigot Chop**[118] with rowan jelly.
- **Aberdeen Angus Beef** either a roast joint or good steaks – and don't forget some good whisky mustard.
- **Steak Pie** warm and filling.
- **Game** grouse or pheasant depending on whether you like a stronger or milder gamey flavour.

Serve any of these in a straightforward way with good Ayrshire potatoes and fresh greens (lightly cooked).[119]

---

[118] *A great Scottish cut of lamb, known as a leg steak in the South. 'Gigot' is one of the many Scots culinary words taken directly from the French thanks to the Auld Alliance.*

[119] *Scotland's history of vegetable cooking isn't great – my dear Great-Aunt Agnes was a school dinner lady and had to arrive at 9am one day a week when it was her turn to put the cabbage on for the children's lunch at noon – we'd have had more nourishment by drinking the water...*

If you are the chef at home, what are the options? I take my starting point from the weather in January – the cauld, cauld wind that blew the gift of poetry into RB usually blows icicles over the rest of us. So let's go for warm and nourishing dishes. This is not a cookery book but I've included a recipe so that, if you want, you can organise your own Supper without having to buy or borrow another book.[120]

If you are minded to have a big pot of stew, you could do something quite simple, warm and filling. It's become a bit of a tradition in our home to have sausage casserole on Hogmanay and at Burns Night. Simple, warm, and you can use your favourite butcher's sausages. Or you could make a traditional beef stew, using a nice Scottish beer. Here's an old recipe which we call Seventy Shilling Stew:

Ingredients

2lbs[121] braising steak (cubed), 1lb small onions in quarters or shallots, 1lb carrots (halved longways), 3 cloves of crushed garlic, dripping (or oil), 1 heaped tablespoon of plain flour, 1 pint of Scottish beer (a nice pint of heavy like Belhaven's 70/-), 1 bay leaf (or thyme), salt and pepper.

Lightly brown the cubes of meat a few at a time and remove to a plate, then brown the wee onions, and lastly stir in the garlic and carrots. Return all the meat to the pan and stir in the flour until it has been absorbed by the juices. Place meat, carrots and onions in a pot on the top of the hob and, adding the beer, bring it to the simmering point while gently stirring. Add the bay leaf or thyme and season at this point and cover, placing in the oven at Gas 4/180C for 2½ hours. Then add a little extra beer if needs be and

---

[120] *Don't worry though, my wife has checked the recipes, so they are edible.*

[121] *Traditional, Imperial measurements without apology.*

adjust the seasoning. After one more hour, remove the bay leaf and the pot lid[122] and cook for a final 15 minutes. Serves four to six.

Sweets and Puddings

Scotland, as any dentist will tell you, is a country that likes its puddings.

The old warhorse is the Scotch trifle. Let's get the naming controversy over with first. This is one of the few acceptable uses of the word 'Scotch' – although nowadays more people will call it Scots Trifle. All tastes the same to me at this point in the proceedings. You'll often hear it called 'Tipsy Laird' which (to be candid) is a late Victorian invention but sounds quite appealing and is, therefore, acceptable on the menu card.

Here's a recipe which we use at home:

Ingredients

12 sponge fingers (left out overnight to go a bit stale), 24 ratafia biscuits, 8oz raspberries, raspberry jam, the rind of a lemon, 5fl oz medium sherry, 15fl oz proper thick custard (no lumps),[123] 1ofl oz cream, toasted almonds or wee sweeties for decoration.

Spread the jam on the sponge fingers and lay across the bottom of your bowl. Pour the sherry over the fingers and leave for an hour. Crumble the ratafia biscuits over the top, sprinkle on the raspberries, then grate the lemon rind there too, before dolloping on the custard. Whip the cream (you could add two spoons of whisky to the cream

---

[122] *You might want to do this the other way around.*
[123] *If you like lumpy custard – tough!*

if you were daring enough!) and spoon it over the trifle in peaks. Sprinkle chopped nuts or sweetie toppings to taste.

Serves eight to ten.

An alternative is to have something really simple such as a bowl of red fruits (strawberries, raspberries, redcurrants and possibility brambles/blackberries) with some Drambuie poured over and a caster of sugar at the side. But the true traditionalist will want to go for one of the great oat-based desserts.

The archetype of the ancient Scottish pudding is Athole Brose, which was made famous when the Duke of Athole[124] served it to Queen Victoria.[125] Take a dessertspoon of runny heather honey, a small glass of fine oatmeal and some cold water, stir together and put in a bottle. Fill with whisky and shake well. Leave for two days. Shake again before serving, possibly with a little cream. Please don't leave the open bottle beside a flame...

If that's too 'in your face' try a cranachan. The easiest form is this: lightly toast a handful of fine oatmeal. Beat some cream and add raspberries until it is pink and stiff. Stir in the oatmeal (not too much) and add a little honey to sweeten to taste. Serve in glasses with a sprinkle of oats and a raspberry on top.

Cheese

Cheese has always been an important part of the Scots dinner. In fact, RB's mother was a noted producer of cheese, using the little milk they had on the farm, and RB mentions it several times in his letters. On the Bill o' Fare at our Supper, the cheese will often be described as kebbuck (the generic word for cheese) an' bannocks (or oatcakes).

---

[124] *Whose ancestor had vanquished his enemies by getting them utterly wrecked with this secret weapon.*

[125] *She was amused.*

There are a growing number of Scottish cheeses available and a cheese board is always an interesting end to a meal. You can have either different colours and textures on a big board or a selection of cuts on small individual plates. I think that, given the Auld Alliance with France, there's nothing wrong with including a bit of French cheese if you want.

The only problem I have is that I am allergic to cheese and so I tend to look on it rather like an American vegetarian looks on the haggis!

My Wife-and-Dancing-Partner is an excellent guide in these matters and her top 10 are:

- From Scotland
1   **Scots Cheddar** from all corners of the land from Orkney to Lockerbie. Classic mild, medium or mature hard cheese. Her current favourite is Isle of Mull, which has a yummy, sharp taste.
2   **Dunlop** from Ayrshire. Creamy and mild like cheddar, but with a sharp aftertaste. Often cloth wrapped.[126]
3   **Caboc** from Skye originally. Cylinders of rich cream cheese rolled in crushed oats.
4   **Arran Blue** from Arran. A blue cow's milk cheese.
5   **Lanark Blue** from Lanarkshire. A sharp blue from sheep's milk. Sometimes called Scotland's Roquefort.
6   **Bonnet** a mid strength goat's cheese, originally from Ayrshire, too.

---

[126] *Especially appropriate, as Mrs Dunlop of Dunlop was a good (if bossy) friend of the poet's.*

- From France
7   **Brie**
8   **Port Salut**
9   **Roquefort**
10 **Camembert**

As an organiser, again the rule is: seek to please your guests within your budget. So whether one special cheese or a selection, choose the best you can afford. In Scotland, the chieftain of the cheese world is Iain Mellis (with shops in Glasgow and Edinburgh) while in England, Paxton & Whitfield are the men. Scotland's love of carbohydrates proves great for the biscuit side of the equation: good oatcakes (rough or smooth) or small bread bannocks. Some people have potato scones lightly toasted (I guess ideal with a goat's cheese or anything at the softer end), while I like to see a traditional rich Abernethy biscuit (the hard to find richer, sweeter digestive – a fine Scottish invention).

As in so many fields of science and the arts, the Scots have contributed well and wisely to the world of biscuits. Messrs McVitie and Macdougall and the redoubtable Tunnock family were forever my happy companions at the tea table. There is a famous tale in the City about the doyen of the biscuit world (would that be the Big Cheese?). Some years ago this famed Scotsman came to London to plan a major transaction with a merchant bank. After a few hours of negotiation on pricing, the bankers called for tea and biscuits. The Scot looked aghast at the plate of biscuits, picked it up and held it at arm's length. 'Are you trying to insult me with these, my rival's biscuits?' he asked, and dropped plate and contents on the expensive Turkish rug. The pricing fell as quickly as the biscuits.

What should you drink with the cheese? Simple answer is a wee bit more (unless driving!). There was a time in Scotland when what you drank after dinner highlighted your political opinions – claret drinkers favoured France, the Auld Alliance and independence, while port drinkers raised their glasses to the Anglo Portuguese and the Anglo Scots links. In Edinburgh in the eighteenth century one could have a brick through the window if the wine store guys were seen delivering the wrong stuff.

Within the etiquette of keeping the last Jacobites happy (see below), there's nothing wrong nowadays with offering a range of fortified wines (including port) and liqueurs (often Drambuie)[127] alongside some good malt. Enjoy!

Coffee

Usually, coffee and/or tea will be offered round. Sometimes on the menu this will be described as 'A Tassie o' Coffee' – a 'tassie' being the Scots for cup. I don't like this as it looks both mean ('a' cup only) and a bit twee. 'Tea, Coffee and Liqueurs' will do. In fact, a lot of folk I know will dispense with the first two.

Tisanes and herbal teas are beginning to be seen in Scotland, but not everywhere.[128]

---

[127] *A whisky and heather honey-based liqueur, the recipe for which was traditionally given by Bonnie Prince Charlie to Captain John MacKinnon of Strathaird, who sheltered the prince in his flight of 1746. To this day Drambuie (from 'dram an budheaich,' the Gaelic for 'the drink that satisfies') is marketed under the slogan 'The Gift of the Prince'.*

[128] *There are some places where if you asked for peppermint tea you'd get a polo-mint on a string in a mug of boiling water...*

Drink

Then let us toast John Barleycorn,
   Each man a glass in hand;
And may his great posterity
   Ne'er fail in old Scotland![129]

If the Scots are not famed as cooks, they have been famed as drinkers for a very long time.[130] I am sure that there are Rechabite and Temperance Burns Suppers as there are Suppers organised by all manners of people, but I always like my Supper to be one that the great man himself would have enjoyed and that, memorably, calls for a dram:

'Freedom and whisky gang thegither.'[131]

---

[129] *'John Barleycorn'. There is an argument about whether Burns is referring to beer or whisky in this poem – it's probably easiest just to enjoy both...*

[130] *While the Inuit peoples are said to have twenty words for snow, Benjamin Franklin famously claimed (after attending a St Andrew's Night Dinner in Philadelphia in 1760) that he would include all 228 words for Scottish Drunkenness in his dictionary. I can't get to that enormous number but, researching the subject with some Edinburgh undergraduates, came up with a list of words in use today. In alphabetical order: awa' wi' it, battered, bazooka'd, beelin', belted, bevvied, birlin', bleezin', blind, blitzed, bloaked, blootered, brainless, deid drunk, far gone, far-on, fleein', floatin', fou, fou as a puggie, full as a wulk, gished, gone, guttered, had a right bucket, hammered, jaiked-up, leathered, legless, mad wi' it (MWI), maroc, miraculous, mortal, on a blinder, on the heavy bevy, on the ran dan, oot the gemme, oot yer box, oot yer brain, para(letic), par-el, p-ed, pie-eyed, p****d, plootered, puggled, reekin', reelin, roarin', rubbered, slashed, slaughtered, steamboats, steamin', stoatin', stocious, tanked, tozy, under the affluence (of inkohol), weill-on, weel gone, wellied, winemoppered, wrecked... No doubt another neologism is being coined in a bar near you right now.*

[131] *'The Author's Earnest Cry and Prayer'.*

We have discussed wines above when planning the menu, but a glass of the 'water of life' is a near-essential part of the celebration. Many of you readers will have more experience of whisky than of other parts of the Burns Supper, but take a few minutes with me to reflect on Scotland's most popular export and the other beverages that will feature at the Supper.

This is the part of the book that will horrify my US readers. How much alcoholic beverage is required for a successful Burns Supper? I recall a FAQ column in the Sunday *New York Times*[132] which suggested that you might have to allocate as much as half a bottle of wine per head to allow the party to go with a swing. I'm not saying that the Scottish Cultural Imperative is driven by booze, but in the UK and Europe we'd tend to see a longer, deeper drinking pattern.

Let me talk to the arrangers for a moment about some technicalities. As with everything, set your plans according to your guests and your pocket.[133] The rule of thumb that we use is a bottle per head plus aperitifs and malt whisky as needed.[134] Let's look at each in turn:

Wines

It's beyond the purpose of this book to give you a detailed look at good fine wines. So I'm going to avoid giving my utterly arbitrary opinion on which wines work with which types of food.

Please feel free to go ahead and enjoy what you like.

---

[132] *But not well enough to be able to find the reference.*

[133] *Or sporran.*

[134] *A very elastic term of measurement.*

Aperitifs

Whether a sit down dinner or a stand up buffet, it's nice to welcome guests with a drink, a nibble and a smile. At the simplest level, the evening starts with a choice of the wines and beers you will be drinking later, while more complex arrangements could revolve around a whisky tasting (with small glasses with three to five different whiskies – and I mean small glasses...). Or you could have something sparkling – champagne or fizzy wine is always a cheerful start to the evening. As a themed touch, I have seen tall glasses of sparkling wine turned into translucent tartan colours by either a drop of liqueur or some simple natural food colouring. A tray full of reds (Kir royale), greens, blues and purples looks very smart.

As with any party, this part of the evening should be relatively short – allowing guests and friends to circulate and meet without peaking too soon.

At Last, the Whisky!

Right, this is a topic that will interest everyone.

Many's the time I've heard arguments over whether Scotland's greatest gift to mankind was golf or malt whisky.[135] I think it all boils down to whether you prefer getting wet on the outside or the inside.

What about the great worry of what should you have in your whisky? The old fashioned answer is 'nothing but more whisky!' There is a strong prejudice against diluting the water of life with the water of tap which is, actually, misplaced. While agreeing that drowning the whisky is a bad idea, most distillers and whisky connoisseurs will admit that a splash of cold spring water at

---

[135] *My good friend Brian McInnes maintains this is a ridiculous argument as it's plainly obvious that both are essential for human life.*

room temperature allows an expansion of the essential qualities of the whisky – try it and see.

One thing on which all parties agree is that unless you are a penguin, you should shy away from ice.[136]

I will focus on the single malt whisky – but that's not to say that the blended whiskies,[137] which make up 90 per cent of total production, don't have their fans too – from Johnnie Walker[138] to Chivas Regal, from the Famous Grouse to Dewars.[139]

There are four main families of malt whisky, sharing characteristics on a regional basis. Here's a quick summary:

Area	Taste	Smell	When to Drink	Popular Exemplar (and an unusual second choice)
SPEYSIDE[140]	Sweet	Pear Drops	Anytime[141]	Glenfiddich The Glenlivet[142]
LOWLAND	Dry and Sweet	Light Grass or Herbs	Aperitif	Rosebank Glenkinchie
HIGHLAND	Round and Sweet	Heather Honey	Haggis	Glenmorangie[143] Highland Park[144]
ISLAY[145]	Smoke, Peat and Seaweed[146]	Medicinal Disinfectant[147]	After Dinner	Laphroig[148] Bruichladdich[149]

[136] *Look at the mess it made of the* Titanic.

[137] *One of the few times you can use the word 'Scotch' is in relation to our whisky. When speaking of the people, 'Scots' is correct.*

[138] *Like Burns's First Edition – hailing from Kilmarnock and still 'Going Strong'.*

[139] *Very popular in the* US, *though completely mispronounced as 'Doo-ers.'*

But the above is at least an oversimplification and like all gener-
alisations[150] is wrong. I hope it at least points you in the right
direction as various healing liquors pass round your table.

As an honoured guest your only worry is whether your glass is
full or empty – but the host has other concerns, so here are some
helpful hints for would-be butlers:

Check for case discounts[151] and special offers.

Consider buying sale-or-return – a good idea if you're not
sure how much to order (for example, a night of bad
weather might mean more people drive and so fewer
drink).

Glass hire can usually be arranged at the time of buying

---

[140] *Speyside is in many ways the heart of the whisky world and afi-
cionados would subdivide this into three or four regions – I'll leave
that to you as homework.*

[141] *Within reason...*

[142] *Founded by J&G Smith – the first guys to go 'legal' and be rewarded
with the patronage of King George IV.*

[143] *Rhymes with 'orange-y'*

[144] *As High in the Land as you can get – this is the northernmost distillery in Scotland, on the mainland of Orkney.*

[145] *Pronounced 'Eye-lah' – sometimes the region is broadened to include
the other Western Isles.*

[146] *Don't let this put you off!*

[147] *Nor this...*

[148] *I must declare an interest, as an ancestor of mine was one of the
owners of the distillery. He perished by drowning in the vats – some
tasters claim to smell a distant top note of old Grandpa Johnston to
this day... Some innocent readers of the First Edition asked if his
first name was Pete...*

[149] *This, and Bunnahabhain are softer, from the northern part of the
island. You know you've had enough to drink when you can say the
names correctly.*

[150] *Including this one.*

the drink – if you have the option, it's usually worth paying a little extra to have the ability to return the glasses without washing them – every little helps on the day after. Remember you'll need more glasses than you think. (One for each wine, one for water, one or two small whisky glasses, and extras for people who lose their glass etc.) You can get away with fewer at a family/small event.

Have a spare dustbin on hand to use for the bottles and cans for recycling.

Have a big bucket of ice (or another bin, or a child's plastic toy box, or even your bath) to keep the drinks cold.

Make sure there's lots of water (Scottish mineral water, of course) and soft drinks[152] – especially if you're planning on dancing after dinner.

Supermarket malts are the excess product from many of the top distilleries, but without the brand, the name or the price tag. Don't feel stupid if you find a malt you like in your local grocery – in fact, get a good book and do some detective work – can you trace it back to its roots?

For a larger, more formal dinner I've seen bottles with the host's own label stuck on. Some of the distillers or bottling companies offer this service.

Have two different malts at the dinner table – a smooth Speyside or a light Lowland with the haggis and a more gutsy Islay for after dinner and the speeches.

A Vac-u-vin or other tool for keeping wine fresh after

---

[151] *For wine, I'm thinking, rather than the whisky…*

[152] *Including Scotland's 'Other National Drink' – Barr's Irn-Bru (We are, of course, the only nation with an indigenous fizzy drink which outsells Coke).*

opening is great if you have a few unfinished bottles at the end of the evening.

Speeches

After the food, or round about the arrival of coffee and liqueurs, the pace of the evening begins to change. You will have spent the last hour enjoying the menu and getting to know your new friends at your table. Now the emphasis moves back to centre stage.

The Queen

> *...I'll give you's The King!*
> *Whoe'er would betray him, on high may he swing!*
> *And here's the grand fabric, our free Constitution,*
> *As built on the base of our great Revolution!*[153]

Many institutions have a tradition of toasting the Queen[154] (or the President of the United States, or your head of state) after the food and before the speeches or entertainment. (In fact some of our US friends toast both the Queen and the President in turn). In Britain, in strictly formal dinners, it was against etiquette to smoke[155] before this point. Now that smoking is banned indoors, I guess the polite convention is that it's rude to nip out for a puff until the comfort break.

---

[153] *'Commemoration of Rodney's Victory.'*

[154] *Often called 'The Loyal Toast', it should always be simple. The chairman should rise with glass in hand and say 'Ladies and Gentlemen. The Queen', pause while all stand and then toast 'The Queen'.*

[155] *Or to take snuff, strictly speaking. I think you can still take snuff indoors under the new legislation, maybe we will see more of it at back tie functions?*

Now we are on truly dangerous ground. In our context of the Burns Supper there are three hurdles to jump.

The Jacobites are the first of these. Some of them are practical adherents who seek the restoration of the UK throne to the rightful heir of the Stuarts rather than a Hanoverian from Germany (although, as the current contender is the Grand Duke of Bavaria, this is rather more complicated that I want to get into), while some are merely wedded to the romance of 'Bonnie Prince Charlie'. Such guests find this toast impossible. At the height of Scottish Nationalism, you would see many guests firmly seated while others rose.

There are some strategies to help smooth this. The traditional route is to make sure that there are jugs of water on the table. Any Jacobite may then rise to toast the monarch and, by passing his glass over the jug at the critical moment, actually toast 'the king over the water' – the exiled Stuart claimant. There is a gender mismatch currently but the principle holds.

Don't worry if your history isn't up to this. The late Pope John Paul II visited Scotland in 1982. At the end of his visit the people started singing 'Will Ye No Come Back Again.' His Holiness asked about the song and was told that it was an old song, collected by Burns, relating to Bonnie Prince Charlie. 'Ah,' said the Holy Father, 'I met his mother at Buckingham Palace last week.'

John Paul II is popularly believed to be the first pope to have visited Scotland. The first reigning pope, certainly, but Cardinal Aeneas Piccolomini (later Pope Pius II) passed through our fair land in 1434, observing:

> The men are short and brave; the women fair, charming and easily won...

> There is nothing the Scotch like better than to hear abuse
> of the English.[156]

Even those who support HM can cause problems here. The second danger is simple to avoid; never call the current incumbent of the throne 'HM Queen Elizabeth II' as many believe her to be Elizabeth I of Scots. The legalities are far too dull and I don't think that there is much chance of a definitive answer but it's one of those fights that certain nationalists love.

Then there are the republican Burnsians. RB's politics are pretty complicated and he has poems both extolling and satirising the royal family on the throne at the time, praising the Jacobites, in favour of republicanism (in the part of George Washington and the French Revolution) and proclaiming the sovereignty of the ordinary man (and the rights of women).

The end result is that, however carefully you plan it, someone will remain seated. Just think of it as one of those complicated family feuds that spark up on Christmas Day over who got Auntie Jennie's second best ring and you'll escape with your sanity.

The one thing that is universally acknowledged is the need to have a short break in the proceedings at this point, to allow the audience a chance to 'stretch their legs', enjoy a 'comfort break', 'make a pit stop', or indulge in some other euphemism for visiting the loo.

When they all come back, the chairman will call everyone to order[157] and introduce the highlight of the evening – the keynote

---

[156] The Secret Memoirs of a Renaissance Pope, *Aeneus Silvius Piccolomini, trans. Florence A Gragg, The Folio Society, London 1988, p29.*

[157] *And in Burns Clubs, will often read fraternal greetings from fellow Burns Clubs, former presidents etc. – a bit like the telegrams and messages at a wedding.*

speaker,[158] who will propose the main toast of the night, celebrating the life, works and genius of Robert Burns in a speech which has always been called 'To The Immortal Memory of Robert Burns'.

The Immortal Memory

Don't let the awkward squad fire over me[159]

The Immortal Memory is the keynote speech of the evening and is a formal and heartfelt toast to the genius, life and works of our Poet.

This is the high of a speaker's career – reputations can be won or lost. I could carry on for years about the nuances and history of this speech, but instead I'll recommend again John Cairney's book *Immortal Memories*.[160] I'll start this thorny subject by talking about formal dinners, and then we can have a look at what you might want to do at home.

How does a speaker approach such a task? What will you expect as an audience? My experience is that IMs fall into four types, each of which is valid. Which is right depends on the mix of the speaker and the audience on that particular night.

The Ben *the speech which takes the high and uplifting approach*

Based on the speaker's personal scholarship, tempered by original and apposite wit, this speech reveals a truth about

---

[158] *In Burns Clubs this speaker is sometimes called 'the Orator'.*

[159] *A Cunningham*, Works of Burns; with His Life *London 1834, Vol I, p344.*

[160] *John Cairney*, Immortal Memories, *Luath Press, Edinburgh 2003. As a young man in Ayr it was a great privilege to be involved in the Burns Festival, through which I met John Cairney – a magnificent and committed performer of Burns, and a memorable one man show, who changed so many views I had on Burns.*

Burns and his work, or discusses one of the key controversies of the Bard's life and/or works, and finishes on a
thought that will inspire the audience.

The Glen *a classic after-dinner speech*

Good old Scots jokes (a happy gallimaufry of golf, whisky
and misers) peppered with quotes and stories from Burns.
This is typically a good natured and amusing way of delivering the speech, carrying little weight of scholarship.

The Highland *an enthusiast's speech*

The speaker's enthusiasm for Burns is captured to explain
and explore a particular trait, or link to a specific group
of people. Humour and a keen ear for Burns are blended
to make a relevant message to the folk in the hall.

The Lowland *the simplest approach*

Often a good one if the audience (or the speaker) is new
to this. This speech takes our guests through the story of the
life and loves of Rabbie Burns with well chosen quotes and
some light moments of jokes. Often a narrative telling the
story of RB's life.

And just to show that I have been on management courses and
managed to stay awake, here's a diagram to illustrate the possible
approaches – potential speakers, position yourself in the correct
quadrant and you won't go wrong!

Speaker's Ability

	GENERAL	INTERESTED	EXPERT
ORATOR	GLEN	BEN	
EXPERIENCED – BURNSIAN			
EXPERIENCED – GENERAL			
NOVICE	LOWLAND	HIGHLAND	

Audience's Interest in Burns

Addressing the concerns and worries of the invited speaker for a moment, I would suggest a few good lines, jokes and stories, but as my friends point out, they all sound pretty old when I say them, so why, dear Reader, should I inflict them on you?

I was taught to speak in a hard school.[161] I'd strongly recommend that you bear in mind two principles and you won't go far wrong:

'Be Yourself' – If you are reading this and are an accomplished, witty and successful speaker you will know what to give of yourself. For the remainder of 'Jock Tamson's Bairns', please be aware of your comfort level in speaking in public. If you know

---

[161] *The Glasgow University Union, recently described by David Stenhouse thus: 'Two Glasgow institutions famously strike terror into the heart of visitors. The audience at the city's Empire Theatre is famous for booing Morecambe and Wise off the stage. The crowd in the Glasgow University Union is even harder to please.' (On The Make, Mainstream Publishing, 2004, p33) I have many (perhaps too many) fond memories of speaking there with Charles Kennedy and others in the '80s.*

that you are no good at telling a joke, avoid trawling the internet and reading an old chestnut.[162] The chairman will have an idea of how long he wants you to speak but make sure that you are happy with that (don't forget that a speech which runs to 15 minutes when you are practising in front of the mirror will last nearly 20 in public).

'Remember Your Audience' – This is particularly true when going abroad – the first time I spoke in Stockholm, I was a bit nervous about my accent and how it might affect comprehension but fortunately the local organiser pointed out that none of my English colleagues had understood me for twenty years – so no point in worrying about the Swedes.[163]

The biggest two criteria to consider are (a) is your audience a knowledgeable gathering of Burnsians who will want a detailed approach, or a more general group who need the basics? and (b) what is the temper of the audience? – there are some Burns Supper audiences that are the latter-day Friday Night at the Glasgow Empire crowd and are famously difficult to control, and others that treat you like the Sunday School teacher. The chairman in this, as most things, is the speaker's best friend – I would counsel some good research in advance.

There used to be a feeling that the Immortal Memory, like a good hellfire sermon, needed to break at least half an hour's length to qualify as a serious attempt. I am more inclined to believe that

---

[162] *Many people try self-deprecation, but I'm not very good at that.*
[163] *Or Turnips (?) q.v.*

the speech should be shorter, and leave the audience wanting more. Many's the time that I've found the last ten minutes of an oration lose the crowd and diminish the effect of both the speech and the evening.

Howsoever you choose to present your speech, at the end, you will make a formal toast, asking those present to fill their glasses, to rise, and with you toast:

'The Immortal Memory of Robert Burns'

At this point, dear Reader, up on your feet with a brimming glass in your hand (it's not obligatory to finish it off in one swallow) and join in the toast with the speaker. Then applaud them!

If we are just at home with a few friends round the table, it's still appropriate to toast the Immortal Memory. A few words from the host or hostess will suffice, but if you're not up for a spell on the soap box you can either propose the toast formally without a speech or, better, read or recite one of the great poems – whichever is your favourite – and toast the man thereafter.

It's your home – do what makes you and the guests comfortable.

The Toast to the Lassies[164]

> *Cease, ye prudes, your envious railing,*
> *Lovely Burns has charms – confess:*
> *True it is, she had one failing,*
> *Had a woman ever less?*[165]

---

[164] *Or, occasionally, 'The Lasses'. I prefer the style I am using but I wouldn't get worked up one way or the other. (Though a couple of correspondents feel very strongly the opposite!) Certainly it's nothing to do with collie dogs…*

[165] *'To Miss Burns'. (Her foible was a habit of taking cash from gentlemen in return for night time favours!)*

As a counterbalance to the weight of the Immortal Memory, the next speeches are a pair – the 'Toast to the Lassies' and the 'Reply to the Toast to the Lassies' – which combine to allow a bit of light hearted banter about the relationships between men and women.

Philosophically, culturally and tastefully, the Toast to the Lassies is a minefield of social indiscretion and political incorrectness. It suffers from many of the problems faced by a best man's speech at a wedding, albeit one with multiple mothers-in-law to keep sweet while giving the boys up the back sufficient entertainment that they don't start throwing food or lapsing into alcoholic coma.

The concept is wonderful. Of all the poets we revere, Burns had a

practical understanding of women, exemplified by the magnetism he radiated. So what could be better than thanking, celebrating and commemorating the fairer sex – in short, toasting them?

I'm going to leave aside the men only or 'stag' dinners in this chapter. This is a thorny topic as there are some traditionalists who believe that this is the only true format[166] – a view I heartily disagree with. (But respect people's freedom to organise their own Suppers as they want.) In a smaller Burns Supper, or if you are just starting out, you could miss these speeches out as they aren't one of the Three Imperatives, but they are good fun!

A couple of very old clubs have a nice tradition of toasting not 'the Lassies' but the one especial in Burns's life – his wife, Jean

---

[166] *Except for the few ladies-only dinners!*

Armour. But that does seem to leave out a large part of his life, so we're assuming here a classic toast-and-reply by a man and a woman in turn.

The strong tradition is that the Lassies is a witty speech – at some point it became a merely funny speech, which declined into a set of puns, and oftentimes now is a prospectus for the retirement home of mild blue jokes.

It should be, dear Reader, 'horses for course'. I have seen, in a male only crowd, clever men weave new material that ranged from the scurrilous to the indecent, with a combination of wit and timing that would make the Moderator of the General Assembly laugh out loud. Those gentlemen are as statistically abnormal as a smile from a London taxi driver. So if you know you can do it and you know that the audience is a willing conspirator, go for it. But under no other circumstances should you rent the video of Chubby Checker or try to put a kilt on www.dodgyjokes.com. A successful Burns Supper is inclusive and it is the speaker's duty to make sure that the message and the humour are appropriate and enjoyable.

So, addressing the prospective speaker: now that all your material has been nicked, what can you do?

There is a good speech to be made out of some 'female' trait or other. I have heard good speeches based round the different kinds of lassies: grannies, mothers, wives, lovers, daughters. There are good laughs to be had over female views on male attitudes. All of these get sprinkled with a bit of Burns's magic dust by quoting one or more of the great love poems.

The rarer approach is to get under the skin of Rabbie's congress with the female sex. This is harder as you have to avoid doing a 'mini Memory' (some of our audience will be quite lectured-out)

– remember you need to capture some humour and sparkle. But when you think on the range and depth of RB's writings on women – that's a huge mine to excavate.

I'll talk about the Reply in the next section, and will repeat this advice there, too (unless the sub-editors get in the way): if at all possible meet up with the Lassie who is replying – the audience finds a matching pair of speeches sweet and it's good to have some friendly 'clash', which best occurs if similar themes or ideas are in both speeches. You can go too far – I have seen and heard Replies which are the second half of the Lassies – there's nothing more worrying than seeing the audience heave a collective sigh of 'here we go again'.

Once upon a time, the Immortal Memory was given in verse (or worse) and quite often nowadays you will still hear a poetic Lassies – but it can be a hard task to bring off – we are seeking, after all, to evoke Rabbie Burns, not William McGonagall![167]

As with all after dinner speeches, your aim should be simple. It's ten times better to have people say 'that was a great speech – we could have had more', than 'he went on a bit…'. I think that the average time for a good light speech is seven minutes (maybe out to ten), so use this length as a guide.

However you craft the speech, its climax is the call to all the men in the room to stand and toast the Lassies. It's a good idea to preface the toast with a quote:

---

[167] *Not that the latter, famed as the Worst Poet in the World, is without his supporters, with the Winers Club of Glasgow holding a February McGonagall Supper these twenty years. The assembled company, all wearing 'bunnets', reach a crescendo of fanaticism during the high-point: 'The Immortal Memory of William Topaz McGonagall – The Poet and Tragedian'. Probably Dundee's second most famous son, after Desperate Dan.*

Come bring to me a pint o' wine
An' fill it in a siller tassie
That I may drink before I go
A service tae my bonnie Lassie.[168]

Then, with a full glass in your hand (or even better a siller tassie – or at least a pewter tankard), ask each and every man in the company to stand, and lead them in toasting 'The Lassies'.

(For the avoidance of doubt, it's only the guys who get up at this stage to toast – Lassies keep your seats – your turn is at hand.)

Now, if you are the speaker, you can sit down to warm applause, with the satisfaction of a job well done, and enjoy what will in all probability be your first (large) drink of the night. If you are a guest, you will have enjoyed a witty speech, and if you are the arranger, you will be well on the way to a successful evening.

Well done all of you!

But it's not over yet... the bell is about to ring for round two.

The Reply to the Toast to the Lassies

O whistle an' I'll come to ye my lad!
O whistle an' I'll come to ye my lad!
Tho' father an' mother an' a' should gae mad,
O whistle an' I'll come to ye my lad![169]

This is the only part of the evening (for apparent reasons) of which I have no active experience. So with the caveat of being an armchair Replier, here's my tuppence to you, dear Lassie, in approaching this part of the evening:

I'd read the section on the Toast to the Lassies first and take on

---

[168] *'To My Bonnie Lassie'*.
[169] *'O Whistle'*.

board any of the principles that seem sensible. You too have to balance the tone between taking the legs off the guy who gave the sexist diatribe (he wouldn't heed my good advice) and being the sweet angel with her giggly thank-yous.

The dingdong is important, and remember that in any give and take the audience love to watch the strop. So I'd specifically repeat a good idea from above: if at all possible meet up with the Laddie who is giving the toast – the audience finds a matching pair of speeches sweet and it's good to have some friendly 'clash', which best occurs if similar themes or ideas are present in both speeches. You can go too far – I have seen and heard Replies which are the second half of the Lassies – there's nothing more worrying than seeing the audience heave a collective sigh of 'here we go again.'

The traditional approach to ending the Reply would be for the speaker to make a gracious (or slightly barbed) thank you to the gentlemen of the company, and the Lassies speaker in particular, and then sit down to applause. Increasingly (and I think quite rightly) the Reply is becoming 'The Toast to the Laddies' with the speaker calling upon her fellow females to rise and toast the Laddies. I rather like this approach – although it causes its own problems in terms of who's driving home.

(Again, all the men in the company remain seated, the better to bask in the adulation of the Lassies – or to cower, beaten – while every female in the company joins in the toast.) In either case it is now time for the speaker to relax to the applause, remembering that she is at least one large drink behind the chap who spoke before.

Well done!

Other Speeches

At a big 'do' there may well be some other speeches, traditional to a particular big event in the social calendar, but at home or a less formal dinner, I think it's better to 'keep your breath to cool your porridge', or at least to add in the singing or reciting.

The big dinner might include:

- The Guests/Absent Friends.
- Scotland (Particularly for expat groups or Suppers beyond the Scottish borders) or 'The Land We Live In'.
- The Society/The University/Our Company etc.
- A formal Vote of Thanks – to speakers, performers, chairman, organiser, Mrs McGlumpher and all…

Very formal and traditional Burns Suppers (sometimes known as Anniversary Dinners in the jargon of Burns Clubs) will have a short 'Appreciation' – a five to ten minute speech by a senior club member who adds his or her critique to support the thesis laid out by the Immortal Memory. While the devotion of the formal Burns Club will support this additional, further call on the audience's attention span, it's not something that I would recommend if it is not already part of your Supper tradition.[170]

In the high Victorian period there would be ten or twenty toasts, 'Auld Ayr', 'The Company', 'The Artistes', or even 'Scotch Drink' – and while they lived 'The Family and Sons of Robert Burns' were regularly fêted (with Tommy Hilfiger proclaiming his descent from RB, maybe this will come back into fashion).

As a general rule, the arranger or master of ceremonies should

---

[170] *Paisley also has the interesting tradition of toasting two other poets – its founder Robert Tannahill and a second Scots poet of the speaker's choosing.*

ensure that these extra speeches are snappy and fairly entertaining as the night is wearing on and, to put it tactfully, attention spans decay in inverse proportion to the depth of whisky in the bottle.

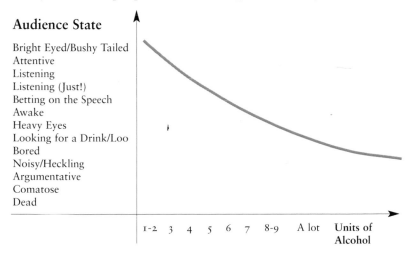

Audience State

Bright Eyed/Bushy Tailed
Attentive
Listening
Listening (Just!)
Betting on the Speech
Awake
Heavy Eyes
Looking for a Drink/Loo
Bored
Noisy/Heckling
Argumentative
Comatose
Dead

1-2 3 4 5 6 7 8-9 A lot   Units of
                                 Alcohol

Music (How many pipers does it take to fill a semi?)[171]

> *A winnock bunker in the east,*
> *There sat Auld Nick in shape o' beast;*
> *A tousie tyke, black, grim, and large,*
> *To gie them music was his charge:*
> *He screwed the pipes and gart them skirl,*
> *Till roof and rafters a' did dirl.*[172]

In a typically playful reference, Burns has the Devil himself play the pipes for the witches' Sabbath seen by Tam o' Shanter. Pipe music has the same central role in every Burns Supper.

---

[171] *Certainly fewer than 'A hundred pipers an' a' an' a''.*
[172] *'Tam o' Shanter'.*

In a perfect world, the guests arrive to the skirl of the pipes and the haggis makes its grand entrance preceded by the piper. At major functions, the Top Table is 'played in' with a solemn[173] procession. And the piper often provides one of the sections of entertainment with a rendition of favourite tunes and dances.

The two things that are immediately apparent when the pipes let rip are the warlike beauty of the music[174] – the great representation of 'Òran Mór' (the primordial song of life in Celtic legend)[175] – and the sheer volume of sound produced (particularly in an enclosed space). A really good piper can give a good blast in an ordinary house without dislodging too much plaster (we are fortunate to have a wonderful guy to play at our home), but in general it is unlikely that you will have a piper playing for you at 100 Acacia Avenue to celebrate your Burns Supper (particularly inadvisable for those who reside in terraces or tenements). So how can you capture this essential Scottish phenomenon at your home Burns Supper?

The easiest way is to use a CD. There is a surprising selection commercially available, which usually hides in 'World Music', skulking between Peruvian Pan Flutes and Finnish Tangos. Mostly the recordings available will be of the Military Bands[176]

---

[173] *'Solemn' has a range of meanings in this context – from the wistful sobriety of the old pro to the blind fear of the new speaker.*

[174] *Truly warlike, for they are the only musical instrument to be defined as a weapon in law. In R v Reid (1746) Lord Chief Baron Parker ruled that 'a Highland Regiment never marched without a Piper and, therefore, his bagpipe, in the eyes of the law, is an instrument of war'. Reid was found guilty of treason and was hanged, drawn and quartered.*

[175] *cf. the 'water of life' – also ubiquitous in Celtic culture.*

[176] *Don't forget that the Royal Scots Dragoon Guards (Caribineers & Grays) were No 1 in the UK pop charts for 5 consecutive weeks in April/ May 1972... amazing! They followed this up in 2007 and 2008 with the wonderful Spirit of The Glen CDs partially recorded by these frontline fighters while on active duty in Iraq.*

but – harder to find but well worth the effort – you can also get CDs of local bands or, better still, solo pipers. You could even get a piper friend along beforehand and record him for the evening (for a suitable artistic reward, I hope).

Have the whole CD playing quite loudly as people arrive for drinks and introductions. (You might move onto something else for nibbles and dinner.) You should choose a good rousing track to bring in the haggis (e.g. 'Scotland the Brave' or 'Heiland Laddie'). Just switch it off when you are done.

If you have room or are simply brave, the alternative is to contact your local pipe band. Most of the members will play at parties for a fixed fee. This can be a nice way to help a younger piper make a bit of honest money and gain some solo exposure. Discuss it with the pipe major or band manager. (For big dinners, the venue usually has a pet piper, and most cities have music managers in the yellow pages.)

The live piper works well outside, welcoming your guests (please agree on the worst climatic conditions he will tolerate – some pipers will play in the rain or cold with a waterproof or overcoat, but some won't). I like it when the front doors (and sometimes windows) are opened to let the music fill the house too.[177]

The Piper will give a quick 'Piping in the Haggis' for you – but do remember that the noise will be phenomenal indoors.[178] In a

---

[177] *It will also fill your neighbours' homes, too – so if you haven't invited them to the party, please warn them in advance.*

[178] *As mentioned, they use a fiddler in Paisley. An accordionist would do.*

larger hall or marquee you have much more flexibility: a solo piper, two or three with a drummer, or the full pipes and drums add a vibrant part of our culture to the evening.

Three points to keep in mind:

1. If you are hiring a piper, agree the terms of service (start and finish times, how long to play, inside/outside, haggis etc.) and fee (inclusive or exclusive of expenses) in advance. Please be generous, particularly if it's a youngster. It's not just entertainment for you and your guests – you are paying for the piper's skill.[179]

2. Everyone has their favourite tunes – but follow the piper's advice. He'll accommodate your requests, I'm sure, but he knows his own range and tempo best – trust him!

3. Make sure the piper receives his ovation from the guests. Don't forget to invite him to share in your drink.[180] He won't expect to join a seated dinner, but if it's a buffet at home you should consider asking him to join you. At big dinners a plate of something in the kitchen is conventional.

From the battle of Bannockburn to the Heights of
   Abraham,
From the plain of Waterloo to the Dargai Hills,
From the fields of Flanders to the beaches of Normandy,
From the heart of Scotland to the centre of your Burns
   Supper –
Cherish and honour the Piper.

---

[179] *Tipping – in the US and Canada, tip the piper like you would a waiter (15–20 per cent). In the UK the fee is usually all-inclusive, but for a good night there's nothing wrong in saying thank you with cash or whisky.*

[180] *If legally old enough.*

Entertainment

The night drave on wi' sangs and clatter;
And ay the ale was growing better:[181]

This concept always worries me. In every book on Burns Suppers the performances are divided into the 'Speeches' on the one hand and the 'Entertainment' on the other. I sincerely hope that some of the speeches are entertaining too! In this chapter I want to explore the performance of poems and songs and other 'turns', whether instrumental or dance.

Poems and Songs

> *But first an' foremost, I should tell,*
> *Amaist as soon as I could spell,*
> *I to the crambo-jingle fell;*
> > *Tho' rude an' rough –*
> *Yet crooning to a body's sel*
> > *Does weel enough.*[182]

In a full dress Burns Supper there will be a poetic performance and a singer placed in between the speeches. My preference is to have songs after the Immortal Memory and a poem between the Lassies and the Reply – that gives a nice balance, particularly if the Immortal Memory is relatively erudite or serious.

The songs are easy – the organiser needs to find a good singer and let them sing. One thing to be careful of, if you are organising, is to be firm on time (see the section on the Chairman/Organiser in Chapter Three) – in most groups one or two songs, possibly with a brief encore, is adequate. Two songs are good as you can mix a slow one and a fast one – simple but effective.

---

[181] *'Tam o' Shanter', line 45.*
[182] *'Epistle to J. Lapraik'.*

The poems are more complex to deliver. Some audiences (and there are Burns Clubs where the members can knock spots off anyone on the platform) like their Burns like their whisky – pure, neat and in large quantities. Other audiences timidly ask for the equivalent of a small Scotch on the rocks.

For the former, a good recitation (never a reading, please) of one of the key poems (such as the great grand national poem 'Tam o' Shanter'), or perhaps a less often heard one ('The Brigs o' Ayr' or 'The Twa Dogs' come to mind) cannot be beaten. Remember, dear Reciter, that the professional audience in Burns Land is as tough as that in the world of opera – the guys in the gods know a bum performance. All I can recommend is practise, practise, practise and take out a good insurance policy.

If you've been doing a bit of research before coming to your first Burns Supper, you might be nervous that the poems need a dictionary or a good translation to understand them. One of the surprising truths of the Supper is that the poems are more accessible when recited – out loud, the cadences of the writing carry those many people who find reading Burns's language challenging. If you find Scottish words or accents difficult to comprehend, just relax and listen to the poem without worrying about every single word. Each time you listen you will hear and understand and enjoy a little more. If time permits, it can be a good idea for the reciter to give a very brief synopsis of the poem, to set it in context (not unlike the programme notes you would find at an opera or musical) and to get the audience thinking about the subject matter.

A more general room might like to hear the good old favourites – 'Holy Willie's Prayer', 'Tae a Mouse' or the like. A great tradition has built up of theatrical performances: excellent recitations given by Holy Willie in his night-gown and cap or the Ploughman with his wee mouse in his hand.[183] For people less familiar with the works (or the language) this is a kind way to contextualise what's going on.

There was a wonderful 'Tam' once in which the reciter had a range of hats and bonnets in front of him, moving from the eponymous Tam o' Shanter, through Kate's cap, the Soutar's nightcap, Auld Nick's horns and Cutty Sark's long hair. It took manual and verbal dexterity but came off well (like Maggie's tail…).

At home, if someone knows a poem (even with the book open) then let them read it at the table. Or you could choose a poem and ask everyone to read a verse. This is a nice way to get everyone active in the proceedings (though please remember that some friends hate declaiming or speaking, so let the book pass by anyone who'd rather stay quiet and enjoy participating as a listener).

Music and Dance

> *Hale be your heart! Hale be your fiddle!*
> *Lang may your elbuck jink and diddle,*
> *To cheer you through the weary widdle*
>   *O' this wild warl'.*
> *Until you on a crummock driddle,*
>   *A grey hair'd carl.*[184]

The pipers have had a whole (soundproofed) section to themselves and we have talked about singing the songs already. This

---

[183] *Go on – be the first to bring in a live mouse as a prop.*
[184] *'Epistle to Major Logan'.*

section looks at button boxes and fiddles and the like, which can both give a turn in the proceedings and provide the wherewithal to dance after dinner.

Formal dinners will usually have one or two musical turns (quite often with a show of Scottish Country Dancing). The real challenge as an organiser is to achieve the balance of the evening. A good fiddler will, like the singer, expect to be allowed two tunes and an encore. It's only fair to give talent its due but it is not a good idea to keep people at their table for too long.

A compromise is to have some informal music after everyone has risen from the tables – either before the dancing starts or accompanying the pleasant promenade round other tables, which affords diners the opportunity to compare notes with old friends. This can work particularly well at home if you have an amateur friend who is half a guest and half a turn.

One of the reasons I am cautious about expanding the running time is that I enjoy a dance at the end of my Burns Supper.[185] This is hard in a big dinner, given the complexities of dismantling tables and making space. The venerable Society of Scots Lawyers in London has a great tradition of serious dancing after its Suppers. It has a hall with a raised platform – the band sits at one end and the dancers fill the rest of the ample floor space. Back at home, why not commandeer

---

[185] *Some Societies are opposed to dancing as they believe that it takes away part of the focus on Burns – but given that we know he liked to dance, and that he spent so much time marrying old tunes to lyrics, I think it's perfectly appropriate.*

the hall or shift the furniture out of the living room? You might even resort to the back garden. With a chum on the fiddle or accordion (or a good CD compilation), you are off to the races.

Dancing is not only great fun (and possibly 'the vertical expression of a horizontal desire'),[186] but a tremendous way to burn off calories and booze. Particularly Scottish Country Dancing, which involves a combination of thoughtful dance steps and the chance to throw your partner about the room.

Now, dancing is dangerous territory. There are dinners which forbid you to step on the dance floor without a certificate saying that you've practised at the sessions in the run up. Certainly more than one career has had a sudden arrest on the Highland dance floor.[187] But with a bit of care and an ear for the beat, most of us – and the tuneless Sassenach,[188] too – should be able to dance some of these:

- The Strip the Willow (which, when danced enthusiastically, is a form of tossing the caber).

- The Dashing White Sergeant (really good as you can get through this one even if only two people out of every set of six know what they're doing).

- The Gay Gordons (an old favourite especially as a good warming up dance even if the name hasn't aged as well).

- The Saint Bernard's Waltz (if your party is keen enough you can be progressive, too).

If you are attending and have little or no idea about what's going

---

[186] *Good old George Bernard Shaw!*

[187] *See David Niven's story in* The Moon's a Balloon, *p120.*

[188] *Commonly this Gaelic word is used as a (slightly pejorative) description of English folk ('Saxons' or 'Southerners') – but strictly it includes lowland Scots, too.*

on, there are a couple of good strategies. In a dance like the Strip the Willow, you and your partner should take position at the bottom (furthest from the band) of a group of dancers – you'll get three or four repetitions before you are the main dancers, which should give you time to pick it up. In pair dances, get on the floor with a couple who know what they are doing and stand behind them to copy (you'll hopefully have someone knowledgeable behind you too, as sometimes you'll end up facing the other way).

If you are attending and do know what to do – please make an effort to dance with someone who doesn't, to introduce them to the dance – I'm sure your other half will do the same.

A good idea if you are planning formal dancing is to have a dance card (or a note on the menu) listing the order of dances. This has two good effects: it lets people plan when to go for a drink/rest/loo break, and it helps ensure that you don't get someone starting the Reel of the 51st when they are supposed to be dancing the Foursome. (Alas! It can happen all too easily.)

A few rules of courtesy:

1   Gentlemen should, strictly speaking, be appropriately attired and should carry their sporran on the left hip. Although this is now probably a bit old fashioned, I am reliably informed that few ladies appreciate the rub of a dead furry beast against their party frock while dancing.

2   Ladies will either have brought little pumps (very keen that – typically seen in those educated by Miss Jean Brodie) or will cast caution and heels to the wind. As Ghillie Brogues are heavy and often steel tipped, please tread gently, lads.

3   It's a bad idea to throw your Strip the Willow partner so hard that she stumbles (and it isn't acceptable to call 'butterfingers' if the next man fails to catch her).

4   No-one ever remembers which side of the set raises its arms at the Dashing White Sergeant, so there can be a bit of stare-down machismo – go with the flow!

5   Don't forget to bow (gentlemen) and curtsy (ladies) at the beginning and end of each dance, remembering to applaud the band (or at home, the CD of the late, great Sir Jimmy Shand).

Auld Lang Syne

Apropos, is not the Scotch phrase Auld Lang Syne exceedingly expressive? There is an old song and tune which has often thrilled through my soul... There is more of the fire on native genius than in half a dozen modern English Bacchanalians.[189]

And of course, one thing that I do not need to tell you is that the evening will close with a rousing rendition of 'Auld Lang Syne', which I suppose is the most sung song in the world.[190] It is also, to every Scotsman's nightmare, the song that's most often sung wrong! Read and memorise the following, please:

---

[189] *Letter, RB to Mrs Dunlop, 17 December 1788.*

[190] *Or possibly, 'Happy Birthday to You,' which we do not sing, even though we are celebrating RB's birthday...*

Should auld acquaintance be forgot,
*   An' never brought to mind?*
Should auld acquaintance be forgot,
*   And auld lang syne!*

For auld lang syne, my dear,
*   For auld lang syne.*
We'll tak a cup o' kindness yet,
*   For auld lang syne.*

An' there's a hand, my trusty fiere!
*   An' gie's a hand o' thine!*
An' we'll tak a right gude-willie waught,
*   For auld lang syne.*

For auld lang syne, my dear,
*   For auld lang syne.*
We'll tak a cup o' kindness yet,
*   For auld lang syne.*[191]

---

[191] *There are three other verses, which are not sung as often:*

An' surely ye'll be your pint-stoup!
*   An' surely I'll be mine!*
An' we'll tak a cup o' kindness yet,
*   For auld lang syne. [Chorus]*

We twa hae run aboot the braes
*   An' pu'd the gowans fine;*
But we've wandered mony a weary foot
*   Sin auld lang syne. [Chorus]*

We twa hae paidl't i' the burn,
*   Frae mornin' sun till dine;*
But seas between us braid hae roar'd
*   Sin auld lang syne. [Chorus]*

I guess there's just less gowan-plucking, pint-stouping and general burn-paidling nowadays...

As with so many of the traditional songs and lyrics Burns collected for *The Musical Museum* and the *Select Scottish Airs*, he captured and rounded the words of 'Auld Lang Syne' – so there are many interesting questions on both the lyrics (how much did RB polish?) and the origins of the music (he certainly recommended another tune as well as that now used). The modern form was widely used throughout the century after his death and became the New Year institution we now know under the baton of Guy Lombardi, the Canadian band leader who used it from 1929 in his New Year's broadcast.

From Hogmanay[192] to Burns Night to St Andrew's Celebrations, and lots in between, this is the closing of any gathering of Scots and their fellows and friends. But what does it mean?

It is a simple song of remembering 'the good old days' in the golden haze of youth or the blue remembered hills of the Highlands. As a title, 'Auld Lang Syne' is as hard to translate as *'A la Recheche de Temps Perdu'*. Literally, it means 'Old Long Past' but the idiom is best caught by something like 'The Days of Long Ago' – expressing that wistfulness so prevalent in Scottish thought and writing.[193]

To ease the blood pressure of purists and wise men, please observe the Golden Rules of ALS:

1   The words 'for the sake of' do not appear and so therefore should not be sung. (While novices[194] may make this error

---

[192] *As we call New Year's Eve in Scotland – and no-one really knows what Hogmanay means. I think it's the future tense of the verb 'to be hungover'...*

[193] *The only other phrases which need translation are 'a cup o' kindness' – a loving cup or toast – and the redoubtable 'right gude-willie waught' – a seriously large drink to one another. I wouldn't order the latter in a contemporary Glasgow pub...*

[194] *Would a novice be a New Auld Lang Syner?*

in ignorance, there are moves afoot to order a community punishment of a bottle of malt whisky to be laid against any experienced Syne-singer who adds these evil words.)

2   'Syne' is always pronounced with an 'S' sound – and **never** with a 'Z'.[195]

3   You start holding hands with the people on either side normally (i.e. your right hand with the person on your right/your left hand with the person on your left), swinging your arms in and out gently. Only at the phrase 'And there's a hand' (which, to be fair, is a reasonably straightforward cue) do you all cross hands (right hand with person on left/left hand with person on your right) with an up and down motion.

4   If you are under 21[196] and on the dance floor it is acceptable that your circle runs in and out in heightening tempo after the hand-crossing.

Three Cheers are sometimes given after the song, and occasionally the National Anthem is sung, but by and large ALS is the signal to your overtaxed body that the night is officially over. Until next time!

Enjoy your sleep. Have a good breakfast. If you are the host, clean up the mess. And look forward, dear Reader, to the next one.

Here's tae us!
Wha's like us?
Dam' few!
An they're a' deid![197]

---

[195] *That's a 'zed' in England or a 'zee' in the States – doesn't matter what you call it – JUST DON'T PRONOUNCE IT PLEASE!*

[196] *Legally or emotionally.*

[197] *A traditional toast, often associated with Glasgow, which I learned too many years ago from Douglas Carson.*

SECTION THREE

Your Duties

And mind your duty, duly, morn and night;
Lest in temptation's path ye gang astray[198]

So that's the running order of a typical Burns Supper. Appendix III gives some estimated running times to help guide you. A good Burns Supper is emphatically not a spectator sport and we all need to contribute to make the evening's magic work. Please let me be slightly bossy and talk about what you need to do to help.[199]

As Audience

The audience is the most important part of the overall chemistry of the evening. There are some notoriously difficult crowds to please.[200] My own rule of thumb, based on my experience as a speaker, is that an attendance of up to 350 will be well behaved, while greater than that sees a noisy minority (about 3 per cent) who need careful management.

Generally the duties of the audience member are seven-fold, regardless of the size of the gathering:

1   To arrive on time, relatively clean and sober and appropriately dressed.

---

[198] *'The Cottar's Saturday Night'.*

[199] *I was originally going to call this book 'A Manual's A Manual for A' That'.*

[200] *Naming no names…*

2   To treat the speakers and entertainers with attention and courtesy[201] and applause.

3   To leave your mobile at least switched off and preferably in a different town for the night.[202]

4   To eat your haggis without whinging (though to be fair to you, you need not accept second helpings).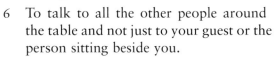

5   To enjoy yourself and make the evening go with a bang!

6   To talk to all the other people around the table and not just to your guest or the person sitting beside you.

7   To not cry out if you lose your bet on how long the Immortal Memory will last (though it should be noted that betting at all is not to be encouraged).

---

[201] *In particular: please keep your seats while someone is performing and don't talk.*

[202] *Trust me, it won't fit in your sporran.*

As Chairman/Organiser

In the good old days, as in modern company law, the regulation and oversight of a Burns Supper was divided between two people – the chairman (or 'preses' in Scots) and the master of ceremonies (or 'croupier'). The former provided the gravitas, the latter ensured the smooth operation of the evening. Today it is rare to have the senior local dignitary in a formal role, so the whole shooting match is on one person's shoulders – *yours!*

Here are the ten rules you need to observe to get through the potential vale of tears:

1   Keep Sober. (Or at the very least, significantly less gassed than the audience). If all goes well, many people will buy you a stiff drink afterwards! (If it goes badly you can drink alone in your hotel room).

2   Ensure that your speakers are comfortable and cared for. At a big dinner, ask your spouse or a friend to help chaperone your speakers. It is crucial to help them mingle, but be sure to rescue them if the town bore traps them in a corner and won't let go.

3   At a small dinner, make sure there's lots of soft drinks for the designated drivers in the company and have a taxi number to hand to give to anyone who changes their mind about foregoing the whisky.

4   Keep the company apprised of what's going on – even if there is a printed programme, introduce every segment and remember to thank the previous speaker or performer and get a round of applause. And make sure everyone can hear what's happening – a poor sound system or bad acoustics have taken the shine off of many a Burns Supper.

5   Prepare your introductions in advance – most speakers

and performers will send a CV (of varying degrees of formality) and there's a lot of information on the web. Check what you're going to say with the person in question (at least in broad brush) and keep your remarks snappy.

6   Arrange brief comfort breaks to avoid having too many people slipping in and out during speeches and recitals, which is a dreadful discourtesy and distraction.

7   Be the most attentive listener, the first applauder and the most pleasant laugher at the oldest jokes. (Similar courtesies include foot tapping to the pipes, clapping in the haggis and being first on your feet at the toasts.)

8   Don't stand any drunken nonsense – if you have a table which is more trouble than the others, a quiet word with the host at a comfort break will often bring on better behaviour, but if the noise of the room is rising, do ask for quiet before each segment. (If remonstrance becomes necessary, I recommend the use of wit rather than physical violence.)

9   You are host of the Top Table too – please be cheerful and friendly with the other guests – they will remember that you have a job to do, but you must still be good to them.

10 Don't forget that when you stand and look round the room, you are Captain of the Ship.

As Speaker or Performer

As one of the 'turns', you will have been contacted well in advance[203] and should have agreed the ground rules with the chairman. I like to get to the venue early to check the layout and the acoustics (particularly if a microphone is needed) and, at larger groupings, to check the sightlines of the tables. People who can't see the stage well are apt to be less engaged, so it's good to know where to put a little extra care.

Beyond the three great Principles of Oratory (Be Sober, Bring your Notes and Don't Forget to Check your Flies) please think of these three other precepts:

1   Know Your Self. Do what you are good at or comfortable with (especially at home – there's nothing wrong with something short). If there is a chairman, make sure that they have your biographical details or know how you would like to be introduced. If you are doing one half of a pair of toasts, introduce yourself to the other toaster. This is good advice, too, for all you musicians, singers and accompanists.

2   Know Your Audience. This is equally true for speakers and entertainers. There are audiences who will love deep and complex speeches and loads of dancing and music, while neophytes really just want a taster to see what's what. Give them what they want and they'll want more next time!

---

[203] *This is a very variable measurement of time.*

If you are performing, weigh carefully whether the audience needs a few, brief words to put what you're doing into context.

3　Know Your Stuff. The themes and contents of the speeches are discussed above – cast your eye over those chapters again. However you like to prepare, give it your whole heart. Research the locality, the club, the chairman – in fact, anything that could make a difference in personalising your work. Use all this wisely and within the allotted timespan!

SECTION FOUR

Variations on a Theme

Life is all a variorum,
We regard not how it goes;
Let them cant about decorum
Who have characters to lose.[204]

There have been many changes in our social customs over the last two hundred years and so different forms of the Burns Supper have necessarily evolved. We can find many novel ways to enjoy this, Scotland's premier celebration.[205] Anything that expands the international circle of people who appreciate Robert Burns and his poetry must be a good thing. I say 'anything,' but would remind you all of the three essential elements of a Burns Supper:

1   A haggis.
2   At least one poem (or song) by the man.
3   A toast (however simple) to Robert Burns.

And who knows? Maybe next year you will try something new at your Burns Supper. Or maybe you'll go to a different sort of event – and enjoy it, too!

---

[204] *'The Jolly Beggars', final chorus.*
[205] *While always honouring the Burns Club Dinner where you will find more knowledge about Burns than in many universities.*

Buffeted by Circumstances

Buffet Thy servant e'en and morn[206]

If you like a larger party and lack a palatial dining room at home, one option is to have a buffet (which is what we have done for years in our home). The general scope is just the same, and can be as informal (or as formal) as you wish.

The evening starts with drinks and trays of hors d'oeuvre using Scottish produce. We have used:

- Mini Scotch eggs.[207]
- Small Scotch pies.[208]
- Cocktail sausages with whisky mustard.
- Smoked salmon or smoked trout on brown bread.
- Venison (or game) pâté on oatmeal biscuits.
- Haddock goujons[209] and small chips[210] (served on a Scottish newspaper).
- Smoked haddock, smoked mackerel or trout pâté, with celery or raw carrots to dip.

After 45 minutes to mingle and eat, the haggis is piped in and addressed with despatch. We bring round plates of little haggis nibbles (perhaps hollowed out small roast potatoes stuffed with haggis, turnip and potatoes or little haggisy meatballs) while putting

---

[206] *'Holy Willie's Prayer'.*
[207] *A hard boiled egg (chicken or quail) wrapped in sausage meat and coated in breadcrumbs.*
[208] *A great delight in Scotland – spicy mutton encased in thin crispy water pastry.*
[209] *Fish fingers, but posh.*
[210] *French fries.*

out the main food (including the big haggis in a bowl) on the buffet table. This works well as everyone – even the shyest – has at least a wee bit of haggis, while the cognoscenti can have triple helpings.

We have a friend say the grace at this point and open the flood-gates to the buffet.

First point to remember: crowd management. The ideal approach is to have two tables, a smaller one carrying the plates, napkins and cutlery[211] (you could use tartan paper plates and napkins and plastic cutlery – if it's good enough for BA Club Class, it's good enough for us)[212] and a second, larger one groaning with food. On a practical note, don't forget that people will lose plates, forks and napkins,[213] so build in extra supplies of everything.

What about the food? A good spread in terms both of amount and diversity is called for. Here's what we had at home last year:

- A big pot of sausage casserole.
- Beef in beer stew.
- Clapshot.
- Side of salmon (poached by our local fishmonger and served cold with a covering of green herbs).
- Vegetarian lasagne.
- Green salad with a simple oil and balsamic vinegar dressing.
- Lots and lots of bread.
- The remains of the haggis with extra mashed potatoes and turnips.

---

[211] *'Flatware', for our American cousins.*
[212] *And a significant saving on clearing up time – have a spare bin/trash can and just clear as you go.*
[213] *You'll find these behind the sofa cushions a year come Boxing Day.*

Our overall philosophy is to have a couple of wintry/meaty things, a fish dish and a purely vegetable bake (both for veggies and vegans and as extra ballast for the drinking carnivores).

Before the pudding comes out, have someone recite a good poem. As everyone else is feeling quite mellow at this stage, it goes down a treat. Then unleash your puddings and cheese. One of our best friends is opposed to desserts at Burns buffets on principle – better to cut straight to the chase[214] and do the speeches with a glass in your hand. While I have some sympathy for this opinion, we tend to put out small glasses of cranachan or a whisky syllabub and a big bowl of redfruits in Drambuie, along with some cheeses and oatcakes.

There will come a point in the evening when even your relatives have stopped eating. That's when the company is called to order by the host to hear the Immortal Memory. We limit this to four or five minutes only, with a formal toast at the end, as that gives us time to have another poem (we know no one who sings outside the sanctity of their own bathroom – but if you have a musical chum then all the better!), or sometimes we choose a longer poem and pass it round the room so that everyone shares in the experience.[215] 'Tam o' Shanter' is particularly suited for this – have a look at Appendix IV, where there are some ideas. One point to remember, please: we all know people who would rather die that participate in 'team games', so let your shy guests opt out with dignity.

Once the toasts and poems are finished, the men clear and remove the tables to the hall, the ladies kick off their

---

[214] *Or the cheese…*

[215] *A bit like* Murder on the Orient Express – *everyone shares the guilt.*

shoes, the kilties swing their sporrans onto their hips and the dancing begins!

We draw a discreet veil over the subsequent morning but I propose one last toast: to the Memory of Mr Bosch (the inventor of the dishwasher!)[216]

---

[216] *Perhaps Mr Barr of Barr's Irn-Bru, too – our other national drink has curiously restorative properties on the day after a Burns Supper.*

St Andrew's Night and Tartan Day

When chill November's surly blast
Made fields and forests bare,
One ev'ning, as I wander'd forth
Along the banks of Ayr[217]

While Burns Night is the pre-eminent celebration of Scottishness, there are many other notable traditions and innovations. Our forefathers would have celebrated the various changes in the seasons: Ne'er Day (1 January), seeing in the new year; Beltane (30 April), the start of the Celtic Summer; Hallowe'en (31 October), which was much more important here than in England;[218] and Harvest Home, marking the end of the agricultural labours.

Particularly amongst expatriate Scots, we find the celebration of St Andrew on or around his feast day of 30 November. This, I am pleased to say, has just been repatriated as the Scottish Parliament has recently voted to make St Andrew's Day a national holiday.

Many of these feasts take the same format as our Burns Supper – an 'Address to a Haggis,' speeches, Scottish songs and entertainments. The difference is that the speeches are not exclusively about Burns (although he certainly deserves a mention). Once upon a time, the other difference was that the main course was not haggis, but a whole sheep's head. Strangely that tradition died out...

The main speech could be entitled:

- Auld Scotia.

---

[217] *'When Man Was Made To Mourn – A Dirge'.*

[218] *It was the Scottish influence which brought this festival into America. Similarly, Groundhog Day comes from our celebration of Candlemas on 2 February. The old Scots tradition about hedgehogs and winter became translated first into gophers and then cinematographically into Bill Murray.*

- Scotland and the Scots.
- The Home Country.
- The Land of Cakes[219] (used at the St Andrew's Society of the State of New York.)[220]

The principles are all the same – good food, good fellowship and an affection for our Scottish culture. So adapt the precepts in this book if you want to enjoy a Supper in the run up to the Christmas season (or any other time that suits!)

An innovation in North America is Tartan Day,[221] celebrated on the anniversary of the signing of what many call Scotland's Declaration of Independence, the Declaration of Arbroath, on 6 April 1320.[222] On the Saturday closest to the anniversary, a

---

[219] *Scotland was known as this in legend – being famous for its oatcakes – and the phrase was captured by RB in one of his poems: 'Hear, Land O' Cakes, and Brother Scots/Frae Maidenkirk to Johnie Groat's' ('On the late Captain Grose's Peregrinations Thro' Scotland').*

[220] *The oldest charitable society in New York. I was honoured (or honoured) to Address the Haggis for the Society's 250th Anniversary St Andrew's Dinner in 2006.*

[221] *In 1991, in response to action initiated by the Clans & Scottish Societies of Canada, the Ontario Legislature passed a resolution proclaiming April 6 as Tartan Day. The USA followed in 1998, when Senate Resolution 155 (S.Res. 155), proposed by US Senate Republican majority leader Trent Lott, was passed unanimously.*

[222] *Many Americans and scholars have noted similarities between the Arbroath wording and that of the US Declaration of Independence. In the original Latin: 'Quia quamdiu Centum ex nobis viui remaserint, nuncquam Angolorum dominio aliquatenus volmus subiugari. Non enim propter gloriam, diucias aut honores pugnamus set propter liberatem solummodo quam Nemo bonus nisi simul cum vita amittit.' In translation: 'For, as long as but a hundred of us remain alive, never will we on any conditions be brought under English rule. It is in truth not for glory, nor riches, nor honours that we are fighting, but for freedom – for that alone, which no honest man gives up but with life itself.'*

parade of thousands of pipers, clan groups, drummers and Scottish institutions, St Andrew's Societies and Caledonian Clubs, and even the unstoppable Tartan Army of Scottish football fans gathers at 45th Street in New York City and proudly marches along 6th Avenue in a colourful and noisy celebration. There are events in other US and Canadian Cities too, notably in Washington DC (on the steps of the Capitol itself),[223] but New York has shown the greatest enthusiasm and the event has grown there from Tartan Day to Tartan Week.[224] New Yorkers and visitors to the city can participate in a gallimaufry of all things Scottish – including the wonderfully punning 'Dressed to Kilt' charity fashion show and a host of parties and dinners. The Vanderbilt Hall at Grand Central even becomes a Scottish village for the week, showcasing Scottish crafts and produce.[225]

Meanwhile, in Burns's own Ayrshire, a vibrant festival has been developed over the last few years. Called 'Burns An' A' That,' it runs for ten days in late May with singers and performers from around the world, comedians, whisky tastings, stars and hopefuls, traditions and innovations. Its formal summit is the Robert Burns Humanitarian Dinner at Ayr Town Hall, where 'an exceptional individual who in the last year has put humanitarian concerns above all others' is awarded a symbolic 1759 guineas and a modern artist's interpretation of the manuscript of 'A Man's a Man For A' That.'

At this rate we will have a Scots party in every month of the year! And the genius of Robert Burns can add illumination to each and every one of them.

---

[223] *Although I wouldn't recommend wearing your Skean Dhu to this particular event!*

[224] *Some in Scotland's political class are trying to rename/rebrand this into 'Scotland Week' but at this time, the Americans are sticking to their guns and Tartan Day it stays.*

[225] *Brigadoon meets Bloomingdale's.*

Hogmanay

So may the Auld year gang out moanin'
To see the New come laden, groanin',
Wi' double plenty o'er the loanin',
    To thee and thine:
Domestic peace and comforts crownin'
    The hale design.[226]

While the celebration of the end of one year and the hope of success and prosperity in the new one is common the world over, the Scots have made it a bit of a speciality. In Scotland there are two bank holidays (1 and 2 January) to allow for a civilised recovery period![227]

There are still many who look to maintain the old traditions of sweeping out the house, inviting friends for food and drink, opening the back door moments before the New Year rings in and, of course, first footing. As the family's fortune is determined by the first person to cross the threshold in the New Year (the 'first foot') you should make sure a tall, dark haired man bearing a lump of coal and a drink is your first visitor. Woe betide you if a short-haired redhead beats him to it, empty handed or not. Let Mr Ginger Hair get in first and you may as well just give up for the next twelve months.

---

[226] *'Verses to Collector Mitchell'.*

[227] *In fact, our holidays remained very different to those in England until quite recently – Christmas Day was a working day, with Postal Deliveries and all, until the very early 1960s.*

Obviously Burns has an influence[228] – in the singing of his song 'Auld Lang Syne' – so why not expand your Hogmanay celebration slightly and have haggis for supper, with a good Address and a brief speech on the year that's been. Sounds like a fine way to end the year, doesn't it? I am sure that RB would raise a glass to that!

---

[228] *Though bringing in the New Year wasn't without its dangers – RB was in Irvine to learn flax dressing and he remembered this party in 1781: 'while we were giving a welcome to the New Year, our shop, by the drunken carelessness of my Partner's wife, took fire and was burnt to ashes; and left me, like a true Poet, not worth sixpence. I was obliged to give up business.'*

SECTION FIVE

A Few Last Thoughts

The Top Controversies

The mair they talk, I'm kent the better,
E'en let them clash;
An auld wife's tongue's a feckless matter
To gie ane fash[229]

We are drawing to a close, and by now there should be few surprises when you join in your next Burns Supper. None of the above is 'holy writ' – only the happy perceptions of one who has enjoyed Burns's work and Burns Suppers in a spirit of exploration and conviviality. But there are some issues which cause 'harrumphs' out loud in the middle of speeches, flames in chat rooms or fisticuffs in bars. Here I hope to tie up some loose ends.

These are some of the things which cause the most heat (and possibly shed the least light) about the man:

1   Which is the largest Burns Supper in the World?

Many websites claim that they represent the largest Burns Supper in the World or that their featured speaker once spoke before the largest. Most such claims should be taken with a pinch of salt (or a large whisky) as it seems that any gathering north of 500 souls is felt to be as big as it can get by the participants.

My vote goes to the Chartered Institute of Bankers in Scotland's

---

[229] *'A Poet's Welcome To his Love-Begotten Daughter'.*

annual London Burns Supper, held in the Grosvenor House's Great Ballroom on the Friday closest to 25 January. The Great Ballroom is the largest room in which you can hold a dinner in London and it's regularly overflowing with between 1,100 and 1,200 guests.

Honourable mentions must go to the Lord Provost of Glasgow's Burns Supper (with over 900 attending in person and many following it online following an innovation in 2004) while Bridgeton Burns Club regularly draws 700 diners and the popular event organised by the West of Scotland radio station, WestSound (over a thousand).

While internationally both St Petersburg and Hong Kong are well known as tartan hotspots; in the USA, I think that the largest Burns Supper in the South is one of the two big Suppers in Houston, TX: The Royal Bank of Scotland's or the Heather & Thistle Club's,[230] while the largest Scottish formal dinner must be the RBS St Andrew's Dinner held for years in New York.[231]

But I expect that someone can prove me wrong on this!

2   Should you sing 'The Star o' Robbie Burns'?

This popular song by James Thomson (words) and James Booth (music) is often heard at Burns Suppers, particularly in Scotland. Some purists feel that only RB's works should be used at the Supper and see 'The Star' as sentimental tosh. On the other hand, if you've ever heard a group of tipsy Glaswegians singing it towards the end of the evening, you'll know it's not all bad.

---

[230] *With about 350–400 heads each. I am biased in favour of the RBS, having been the guest speaker and master of ceremonies there every year since it was founded by Kevin Howard in 2000.*

[231] *Started by Graham Broyd in 2001, its largest sitting was 700 guests.*

The Star o' Robbie Burns

There is a star whose beaming ray
is shed on ev'ry clime. It shines by night, it shines by day
An' ne'er grows dim wi' time.
It rose upon the banks of Ayr,
It shone on Doon's clear stream –
A hundred years are gane and mair,
Yet brighter grows its beam.
> *[Chorus]*
> *Let kings and courtiers rise and fa',*
> *This world has mony turns*
> *But brightly beams aboon them a'*
> *The star o' Robbie Burns.*

Though he was but a ploughman lad
An' wore the hodden grey,
Auld Scotland's sweetest bard was bred
Aneath a roof o' strae.
To sweep the strings o' Scotia's lyre,
It needs nae classic lore;
It's mither wit an native fire
That warms the bosom's core.

> *[Chorus]*

On fame's emblazon'd page enshrin'd
His name is foremost now,
An' many a costly wreath's been twin'd
To grace his honest brow.
An' Scotland's heart expands wi' joy
Whene'er the day returns
That gave the world its peasant boy
Immortal Robbie Burns.

3 Do I call him 'Rabbie' or 'Robbie' Burns?

RB was as heterodox in what he called himself as he was in most things. You'll remember that he changed the spelling of his surname from his father's Kincardineshire 'Burnes' to the more Ayrshire 'Burns'. He was pretty flexible on his Christian name, too.

If there is a brick that's often heaved at our American friends, it's the question 'why do they call him 'Robbie' Burns or 'Bobbie' Burns?' The hardliners among us would opine that 'Robbie' = Williams and 'Bobbie' = Socks and neither should be used in connection with the Bard.[232]

But maybe we are too prejudiced. Look at how Burns signed himself:

- Rab (or Rab the Rhymer or Rab Mossgeil after his farm)
- Rob
- Rantin' Rovin' Robin
- Rob't Burns
- Robert Burns
- Robert Burnes, in his youth

Oddly enough, two formulations he never used were 'Rabbie' and 'Robbie'.

4 Where do you put your whisky at the haggis course?

Inside you. How it gets there is between you and your conscience (or at least your digestion).

Drink it while you eat your haggis or pour it over the haggis like a sauce. My preference is for the former, but to each his own on this

---

[232] *Of course, the sharp-eyed amongst you will have noticed the use of 'Robbie' in 'The Star' above.*

one. Do be careful though not to use your host's £250 limited edition, Madeira cask, single vat malt for any purpose but imbibing!

5   Can you tell a 'blue' joke in the Lassies speech?

Never.

In fact, not as frequently as that.

There have been a few outstanding speakers who can make a funny, risqué speech (in another field, I think of the late Bob Monkhouse, who is the only man I've ever heard of to have his joke books stolen and held to ransom). From the speaker's perspective it's asymmetric warfare – the people who will be offended will be more offended than the people who will be amused will be amused. Open the oven door to check on a soufflé before it's ready and you'll get the net effect.

6   How many children did Robert Burns father?

Burns's poetic fecundity was matched only by his sexual virility. There is a lot of boo/hiss argument about this aspect of his life – with the cheers from those who see the simple satisfaction of sexuality without hypocrisy matched by the jeers of those who see this as a fatal weakness or selfishness. Both sides get pasted by those who believe that there is too much focus on the man, and not enough on his work.

That being said, since you asked the question, RB is officially known to have had twelve children with four different women. I've marked the illegitimate births with a ♥, the children who died before him with a ♣, and his posthumous son with a ♦.

Jean Armour

Robert ❤ [233] and Jean ❤ ♣

Unnamed twin girls ❤ ♣

Francis Wallace

William Nicol

Elizabeth Riddell ♣

James Glencairn

Maxwell ♦

Elizabeth Paton

Elizabeth ('Bess') ❤

Jennie Clow

Robert ❤

Anna Park

Elizabeth ('Betty') ❤

This is somewhat subject to revision as there are many tall, dark haired Ayrshire men whose great grannies are a bit shy about their antecedents. There are two anomalies which deserve mention. Meg Cameron took out a paternity writ against RB, who settled it, but we know nothing about the baby (not even if it was born or not). This could well have been a thirteenth child for RB.[234] I do not believe that 'Highland Mary' Campbell was pregnant, although there are many who believe otherwise.

I'd give a grand total of thirteen children by five women.

7   When can you hold a Burns Supper?

As we all know, Burns was born on 25 January 1759 (although due to an error by Dr Currie, the first biographer, the date was thought to be 29 January for many years – amazing when you think of the pretty definitive lyrics of 'There was a Lad').[235] So the basic answer is – *the* date is 25 January annually.

---

[233] *My sincere apologies as I accidentally killed off Robert Jr in the First Edition. Not a very fraternal thing to do to a fellow Glasgow Alumnus.*

[234] *It was at least a pregnancy.*

[235] *'Oor Monarch's hinmost year but yin,*
Was five-and-twenty days begun'

A number of the early societies and clubs commemorated the date of his death instead – July 21 – but everyone seems to enjoy the birthday more than the wake.[236]

Given the exigencies of the modern word, your Burns Supper will often be held on the nearest Thursday, Friday or Saturday to 25 January. There is a bit of a log-jam, however, with many conflicting Suppers, so in practice the 'season' runs from after just after Twelfth Night (Old Christmas Day or Hansel Day) through to the end of February. That's good news for all of us who enjoy a good Burns Supper and rather excellent news for those of us who get paid to speak!

---

[236] *Mind you, a good Scots funeral is as much fun as you can get for free... As the old Ayrshire saying goes: you should always go to a funeral – if you don't go to theirs, they won't come to yours.*

Having Fun!

Care, mad to see a man sae happy,
E'en drown'd himself amang the nappy.   [beer]
As bees flee hame wi' lades o' treasure,
The minutes wing'd their way wi' pleasure:
Kings may be blest but Tam was glorious,
O'er a' the ills o' life victorious! [237]

So here we are, dear Reader, at the end of the book. No more typing for me, and no more reading for you. [238]

If you are attending a Burns Supper for the first time, or have been before and wondered 'why?' at some point in the evening, I hope that the preceding pages have explained this unique phenomenon and added (or will add) to your fun. A good Burns Supper creates a community amongst those present, based in equal parts on the conviviality of good company, the joy of fine Scottish food and drink, and the insight into our essential humanity captured by the songs and poems of one of the greatest Bards of any time in any language.

If you are one of the lucky people due to perform Burns's works or speak in his praise, I hope this has clarified your task and given you some good ideas about how to bring off an effective performance which will engage your audience, even if they have had little exposure to Burns. Perhaps you can even make some of the experts think again.

If you are thinking about arranging a Supper, I hope this wee book has encouraged you to do so. Whether it's you and your family round the kitchen table or you are master of ceremonies

---

[237] *'Tam o' Shanter'.*
[238] *And I've run out of famous people to name drop in my footnotes...*

to 700 bow-tied guests, the principles of having fun are identical. I mentioned them at the beginning, but it's well worth a reprise:

- Have as many or as few people as you want to invite.
- Have as much food and drink as you can afford.
- Have as much or as little formality as you all feel comfortable with (but don't forget the three essential elements: a haggis, a poem and a toast to Robert Burns).

The Burns Supper is the greatest, largest, noisiest popular celebration of literature, utterly spontaneous and spanning the world – so why don't you share in it this year?

Let me end, as is only right, with a poem from RB which, for me, gives all the elements of a Burns Supper in verse:

AT WHIGHAM'S INN, SANQUHAR

Envy, if thy jaundiced Eye
Through this window chance to spy,
To thy sorrow thou shalt find,
All that's generous, all that's kind.
Friendship, virtue, every grace,
Dwelling in this happy place.

Appendix 1

'Address to a Haggis' – A new verse translation

Address to a Haggis

By Robert Burns

A new verse translation
by Clark McGinn

Fair fa' your honest, sonsie face,
Great chieftain o' the puddin-race!
Aboon them a' ye tak your place,
Painch, tripe, or thairm:
Weel are ye wordy of a grace
As lang's my arm.

The groaning trencher there ye fill,
Your hurdies like a distant hill,
Your pin wad help to mend a mill
In time o' need,
While thro' your pores the dews distil
Like amber bead.

His knife see rustic Labour dight,
An' cut ye up wi' ready slight,
Trenching your gushing entrails bright,
Like onie ditch;
An' then, O what a glorious sight,
Warm-reeking, rich!

Then horn for horn, they stretch an' strive:
Deil tak the hindmost, on they drive,
Till a' their weel-swall'd kytes belyve
Are bent like drums;
Then auld Guidman, maist like to rive,
'Bethankit!' hums.

You've an honest, round and jolly face,
Great chieftain of the sausage race!
Above them all you take your place,
Offal, tripe or lamb:
You are most worthy of a grace
As long's my arm.

The groaning platter there you fill,
Your buttocks like a distant hill,
Your skewer could help mend a mill
In time of need,
While through your pores the dews distil
Like amber bead.

His knife is wiped with rustic might,
To cut you up with ready sleight,
Digging up gushing entrails bright,
Like out a ditch;
And then, O what a glorious sight,
Warm, steaming, rich!

Then spoon for spoon, they stretch out fast:
On they drive – Hell take the last,
Till all the swollen guts so vast
Are tight as drums;
Then old Grandpa, most fit to burst,
'Thanks Be!' he hums.

Is there that owre his French ragout,
Or olio that wad staw a sow,
Or fricassee wad mak her spew
Wi' perfect scunner,
Looks down wi' sneering, scornfu' view
On sic a dinner?

Poor devil! See him owre his trash,
As feckless as a wither'd rash,
His spindle shank a guid whip-lash,
His nieve a nit;
Tho' bluidy flood or field to dash,
O how unfit!

But mark the Rustic, haggis-fed,
The trembling earth resounds his tread,
Clap in his walie nieve a blade,
He'll make it whistle;
An' legs, an' arms, an' heads will sned
Like taps o' thrissle.

Ye pow'rs, wha mak mankind your care,
An' dish them out their bill o' fare,
Auld Scotland wants nae skinking ware,
That jaups in luggies;
But if ye wish her gratfu' prayer,
Gie her a Haggis!

Who, with a plate of French ragout,
Or pig-sickening oily stew,
Or fricassee to make you throw
With real distaste,
Looks down with sneering, scornful view
On such a feast?

Poor devil! See him eat his trash,
As feeble as a withered rush,
His skinny legs a mere whip-lash,
His fist a nut;
Through bloody flood or field to dash,
O how unfit!

But mark the Rustic, haggis-fed,
The trembling earth resounds his tread,
His big fist holds a knife of dread,
He'll make it whistle;
Chopping legs, arms, and every head
Like tops of thistle.

You powers, who make mankind your care,
And dish them out their bill of fare,
Old Scotland wants no soupy ware,
To splosh in dishes;
But if you wish her grateful prayer,
Give her a Haggis!

Appendix II

Helpful Websites

You can't blame a boy for a bit of self-promotion, so here is my own website:

www.seriousburns.com

Although this book is pretty self-sufficient as it gives you all the information you need to start organising Burns Suppers willy-nilly, you will want to expand your experience. Here, therefore, are a few specialist websites about RB:

The Robert Burns World Federation
  www.worldburnsclub.com

The Global Burns Network
  www.gla.ac.uk/globalburnsnetwork

Burns An' A' That Festival
  www.burns.visitscotland.com/festival

Robert Burns National Heritage Park
  www.burnsheritagepark.com

John Cairney – The Man Who Played Robert Burns
  www.johncairney.com

The Centre for Robert Burns Studies
  www.gla.ac.uk/departments/scottishliterature/robertburnscentre

Scotland Now
  www.friendsofscotland.gov.uk/scotlandnow/issue-16/index.html

And for all you Scots in London and its environs, there is the great and growing community called 'Scots in London'
  www.scotsinlondon.com

Appendix III

Sample Running Order

As in so many parts of the human comedy, timing is everything in arranging a Burns Supper. Here is a quick outline of the timeline for a big dinner, and also for a wee dinner:

	THE BIG DINNER	THE WEE DINNER
7.00	Guests arrive – aperitifs and canapés[239]	Probably people will be invited for 7.30 – but chums might come earlier…
7.30	Guests are summoned to sit down (Five minutes earlier if the Top Table are to enter in procession)	
7.35	Chairman's welcoming remarks (*brief*!)	Drinks and chat
7.40	Grace	Either sit down for a starter (already on the table), or if it's a buffet start handing round nibbles
7.45	Starter course (possibly already on the table)	Grace
8.05	Chairman introduces the Haggis Addressor	Host warns of the arrival of the haggis, which is 'piped' in.
8.08	Haggis Addressor's preliminary remarks (optional)	If a buffet, you'll need a wee table to put the haggis on
8.12	Haggis piped in	

---

[239] *Or drinks and nibbles.*

8.17	Haggis on the table	Haggis on the table
	'Address to a Haggis'	'Address to a Haggis'
8.25	Toast the haggis	Toast the haggis
	piper/haggis leave	piper/haggis leave
8.30	Serve the haggis course	Serve the haggis at the table – or put it onto the buffet
8.45	Main course	Main course
9.10	Desserts and coffee (Toast to the Queen can be here)	Desserts and coffee
9.20	Comfort break	
9.30	Chairman's welcome to the Speakers and Entertainers	Host gives a quick plan of the events
9.35	The Immortal Memory	A short Immortal Memory
10.00	Standing ovation (!)	or even just a toast to RB – 10 mins
10.05	Songs or Poems	Songs or Poems Maybe The Lassies/Laddies or one short funny toast to Jean Armour
10.15	The Lassies	
10.25	The Reply to the Lassies	The remaining informal,
10.35	Entertainment	convivial evening with maybe a dance or two...
10.50	Chairman/Vote of Thanks	
10.55	Auld Lang Syne	
11.00	Finish/Go to the bar/Dancing begins	

Appendix IV

Some of the Great Poems for Reciting

As this book aims to give you the wherewithal to hold a complete Burns Supper, here are a few of the poems which you and your friends can recite. I'd heartily recommend buying a book of the poems (it needn't cost much as there are a number of cheap paperback editions to set you off).

I've tried to capture the breadth and depth of RB's work. These are the poems I recommend. I have neither translated them nor annotated them, but I have given an overview here which will help you understand them.

- 'To A Mouse' – as the ploughman upsets a mouse's nest while ploughing his fields, he reflects on the link between man and nature, and the things in the future which may upset his life.

- 'Holy Willie's Prayer' – a sparkling and ironic attack at hypocrisy – great comedy. The introduction by Burns explains the feud between the poet's friend and the church elder out to get him. RB imagines overhearing Willie confess his own sins, being sure that the Lord will save him.

- 'My Love is Like A Red, Red Rose' – either sung or recited, one of the most potent love lyrics – written to Jean Armour

- 'A Man's A Man For A' That' – the essential philosophy of the community of humankind

- 'Tam o' Shanter' – RB's greatest achievement – one of the finest narrative poems in literature – capturing wit, joy, boozing, love, the supernatural and more. This is ideal to use as a 'round robin'[240] by passing the book round the table to let every guest have a share in the performance.

♦   The poem opens on market day in Ayr, where Tam, a farmer from out in the country, and his best friend the cobbler (Souter Johnnie) are getting happily blootered while Tam's wife waits to get her hands on him.

♦   At midnight, with a storm raging, he has to ride home on Meg his old mare (who is pretty used to finding her own way home while Tam is drunk). Tam gets increasingly nervous in the thunder and lightning.

♦   He sees Alloway Kirk full of light – and on creeping up, is horrified to see a witches' Sabbath in progress with the Devil piping tunes for witches and warlocks to dance old Scottish country reels.

♦   Befuddled by drink, he sees one very pretty witch whose shroud is too short – Tam calls out 'Well done Cutty Sark!'[241] (Well done you with the short skirt!) and the hellish host gathers against him.

♦   Fortunately Meg has her breath back and goes full pelt for home – but Cutty Sark is faster than the others and presses close upon Tam who, with impeccable timing, reaches the bridge just as Cutty Sark catches Meg's tail – the witch cannot cross running water, but Meg loses her tail while Tam gains a lesson!

---

[240] *Or maybe a 'Rantin' Rovin' Robin'?*

[241] *The famous clipper show now moored at Greenwich is named after the witch and you can see her today as the figurehead, fairly ample in curvature, quite low on clothing and proudly beating a horse's tail on her hand! Interestingly, I was reminded by Murray that, just as the witch came second in the race with Maggie, the* Cutty Sark *is only the second fasted clipper ship, having been beaten by the* Thermopylae *(14 knots for 24 hours in 1878).*

To A Mouse

*On Turning Her Up In Her Nest With The Plough, November,
1785*

Wee, sleekit, cow'rin, tim'rous beastie,
O, what a panic's in thy breastie!
Thou need na start awa sae hasty,
Wi' bickering brattle!
I wad be laith to rin an' chase thee,
Wi' murd'ring pattle!

I'm truly sorry man's dominion,
Has broken nature's social union,
An' justifies that ill opinion,
Which makes thee startle
At me, thy poor, earth-born companion,
An' fellow-mortal!

I doubt na, whiles, but thou may thieve;
What then? poor beastie, thou maun live!
A daimen icker in a thrave
'S a sma' request;
I'll get a blessin wi' the lave,
An' never miss't!

Thy wee bit housie, too, in ruin!
It's silly wa's the win's are strewin'!
An' naething, now, to big a new ane,
O' foggage green!
An' bleak December's winds ensuin,
Baith snell an' keen!

Thou saw the fields laid bare an' waste,
An' weary winter comin fast,
An' cozie here, beneath the blast,
Thou thought to dwell –
Till crash! the cruel coulter past
Out thro' thy cell.

That wee bit heap o' leaves an' stibble,
Has cost thee mony a weary nibble!
Now thou's turn'd out, for a' thy trouble,
But house or hald,
To thole the winter's sleety dribble,
An' cranreuch cauld!

But, Mousie, thou art no thy lane,
In proving foresight may be vain;
The best-laid schemes o' mice an' men
Gang aft agley,
An' lea'e us nought but grief an' pain,
For promis'd joy!

Still thou art blest, compar'd wi' me
The present only toucheth thee:
But, Och! I backward cast my e'e.
On prospects drear!
An' forward, tho' I canna see,
I guess an' fear!

This theme was famously the inspiration for John Steinbeck's 'Of Mice and Men'.

Holy Willie's Prayer

'And send the godly in a pet to pray.' – Pope.[242]

Argument

Holy Willie was a rather oldish bachelor elder, in the parish of Mauchline, and much and justly famed for that polemical chattering, which ends in tippling orthodoxy, and for that spiritualised bawdry which refines to liquorish devotion. In a sessional[243] process with a gentleman in Mauchline – a Mr Gavin Hamilton – Holy Willie and his priest, Father Auld, after full hearing in the presbytery of Ayr,[244] came off but second best; owing partly to the oratorical powers of Mr Robert Aiken, Mr Hamilton's counsel; but chiefly to Mr Hamilton's being one of the most irreproachable and truly respectable characters in the county. On losing the process, the muse overheard him [Willie] at his devotions, as follows: –

O Thou, who in the heavens does dwell,
Who, as it pleases best Thysel',
Sends ane to heaven an' ten to hell,
A' for Thy glory,
And no for ony gude or ill
They've done afore Thee!

---

[242] *These are RB's own epigraph and explanation of the controversy which inspired the poem.*
[243] *The Kirk Session is the body of the Minister and Elders which governs a parish in the Church of Scotland and which is responsible for the discipline of the congregation.*
[244] *The Presbytery is the regional governing body in the Kirk, where the Minister and one elder from every Session join in the oversight of the county, including hearing appeals from individual sessions.*

I bless and praise Thy matchless might,
When thousands Thou hast left in night,
That I am here afore Thy sight,
For gifts an' grace
A burning and a shining light
To a' this place.

What was I, or my generation,
That I should get sic exaltation,
I wha deserve most just damnation
For broken laws,
Sax thousand years ere my creation,
Thro' Adam's cause?

When frae my mither's womb I fell,
Thou might hae plunged me in hell,
To gnash my gums, to weep and wail,
In burnin lakes,
Where damned devils roar and yell,
Chain'd to their stakes.

Yet I am here a chosen sample,
To show thy grace is great and ample;
I'm here a pillar o' Thy temple,
Strong as a rock,
A guide, a buckler, and example,
To a' Thy flock.

O Lord, Thou kens what zeal I bear,
When drinkers drink, an' swearers swear,
An' singin there, an' dancin here,
Wi' great and sma';
For I am keepit by Thy fear
Free frae them a'.

But yet, O Lord! Confess I must,
At times I'm fash'd wi' fleshly lust:
An' sometimes, too, in wardly trust,
Vile self gets in:
But Thou remembers we are dust,
Defil'd wi' sin.

O Lord! yestreen, Thou kens, wi' Meg –
Thy pardon I sincerely beg,
O! may't ne'er be a livin' plague
To my dishonour,
An' I'll ne'er lift a lawless leg
Again upon her.

Besides, I farther maun allow,
Wi' Leezie's lass, three times I trow –
But Lord, that Friday I was fou,
When I cam near her;
Or else, Thou kens, Thy servant true
Wad never steer her.

Maybe Thou lets this fleshly thorn
Buffet Thy servant e'en and morn,
Lest he owre proud and high shou'd turn,
That he's sae gifted:
If sae, Thy han' maun e'en be borne,
Until Thou lift it.

Lord, bless Thy chosen in this place,
For here Thou hast a chosen race:
But God confound their stubborn face,
An' blast their name,
Wha bring Thy elders to disgrace
An' public shame.

Lord, mind Gaw'n Hamilton's deserts;
He drinks, an' swears, an' plays at cartes,
Yet has sae mony takin' arts,
Wi' great and sma',
Frae God's ain priest the people's hearts
He steals awa.

An' when we chasten'd him therefor,
Thou kens how he bred sic a splore,
An' set the warld in a roar
O' laughing at us;
Curse Thou his basket and his store,
Kail an' potatoes.

Lord, hear my earnest cry and pray'r,
Against that Presbyt'ry o' Ayr;
Thy strong right hand, Lord, make it bare
Upo' their heads;
Lord visit them, an' dinna spare,
For their misdeeds.

O Lord, my God! that glib-tongu'd Aiken,
My vera heart and flesh are quakin',
To think how we stood sweatin', shakin',
An' piss'd wi' dread,
While he, wi' hingin' lip an' snakin',
Held up his head.

Lord, in Thy day o' vengeance try him,
Lord, visit them wha did employ him,
And pass not in Thy mercy by 'em,
Nor hear their pray'r,
But for Thy people's sake, destroy 'em,
An' dinna spare.

But, Lord, remember me an' mine
Wi' mercies temp'ral an' divine,
That I for grace an' gear may shine,
Excell'd by nane,
And a' the glory shall be thine,
Amen, Amen!

My Love is Like a Red, Red Rose

O my Luve's like a red, red rose,
That's newly sprung in June:
O my Luve's like the melodie,
That's sweetly play'd in tune.

As fair art thou, my bonie lass,
So deep in luve am I;
And I will luve thee still, my dear,
Till a' the seas gang dry.

Till a' the seas gang dry, my dear,
And the rocks melt wi' the sun;
And I will luve thee still, my dear,
While the sands o' life shall run.

And fare-thee-weel, my only Luve!
And fare-thee-weel, a while!
And I will come again, my Luve,
Tho' 'twere ten thousand mile!

It was a joy to learn from my friends in Stockholm that one of the most popular songs in Swedish – 'Min älskling' by Evert Taube is, in fact, a translation of this lovely Burns song.

A Man's A Man For A' That

Is there for honest Poverty
That hings his head, an' a' that;
The coward slave – we pass him by,
We dare be poor for a' that!
For a' that, an' a' that.
Our toils obscure an' a' that,
The rank is but the guinea's stamp,
The Man's the gowd for a' that.

What though on hamely fare we dine,
Wear hoddin grey, an' a' that;
Gie fools their silks, and knaves their wine;
A Man's a Man for a' that:
For a' that, and a' that,
Their tinsel show, an' a' that;
The honest man, tho' e'er sae poor,
Is king o' men for a' that.

Ye see yon birkie, ca'd a lord,
Wha struts, an' stares, an' a' that;
Tho' hundreds worship at his word,
He's but a coof for a' that:
For a' that, an' a' that,
His ribband, star, an' a' that:
The man o' independent mind
He looks an' laughs at a' that.

A prince can mak a belted knight,
A marquis, duke, an' a' that;
But an honest man's abon his might,
Gude faith, he maunna fa' that!
For a' that, an' a' that,
Their dignities an' a' that;
The pith o' sense, an' pride o' worth,
Are higher rank than a' that.

Then let us pray that come it may,
(As come it will for a' that,)
That Sense and Worth, o'er a' the earth,
Shall bear the gree, an' a' that.
For a' that, an' a' that,
It's coming yet for a' that,
That Man to Man, the world o'er,
Shall brothers be for a' that.

Tam o' Shanter

A Tale. 'Of Brownyis and of Bogillis full is this Buke.' Gawin Douglas.

When chapman billies leave the street,
And drouthy neibors, neibors, meet;
As market days are wearing late,
An' folk begin to tak the gate,
While we sit bousing at the nappy,
An' getting fou and unco happy,
We think na on the lang Scots miles,
The mosses, waters, slaps and stiles,
That lie between us an' our hame,
Where sits our sulky, sullen dame,
Gathering her brows like gathering storm,
Nursing her wrath to keep it warm.

This truth fand honest Tam o' Shanter,
As he frae Ayr ae night did canter:
(Auld Ayr, wham ne'er a town surpasses,
For honest men and bonie lasses).

O Tam! Had'st thou but been sae wise,
As taen thy ain wife Kate's advice!
She tauld thee weel thou was a skellum,
A blethering, blustering, drunken blellum;
That frae November till October,
Ae market-day thou was na sober;
That ilka melder wi' the Miller,
Thou sat as lang as thou had siller;
That ev'ry naig was ca'd a shoe on
The Smith and thee gat roarin' fou on;
That at the Lord's house, ev'n on Sunday,

Thou drank wi' Kirkton Jean till Monday,
She prophesied that late or soon,
Thou wad be found, deep drown'd in Doon,
Or catch'd wi' warlocks in the mirk,
By Alloway's auld, haunted kirk.

Ah, gentle dames! it gars me greet,
To think how mony counsels sweet,
How mony lengthen'd, sage advices,
The husband frae the wife despises!

But to our tale: Ae market night,
Tam had got planted unco right,
Fast by an ingle, bleezing finely,
'Wi reaming swats, that drank divinely;
And at his elbow, Souter Johnnie,
His ancient, trusty, drouthy crony:
Tam lo'ed him like a very brither;
They had been fou for weeks thegither.
The night drave on wi' sangs an' clatter;
And aye the ale was growing better:
The Landlady and Tam grew gracious,
Wi' favours secret, sweet, and precious:
The Souter tauld his queerest stories;
The Landlord's laugh was ready chorus:
The storm without might rair and rustle,
Tam didna mind the storm a whistle.
Care, mad to see a man sae happy,
E'en drown'd himsel amang the nappy.
As bees flee hame wi' lades o' treasure,
The minutes wing'd their way wi' pleasure:
Kings may be blest, but Tam was glorious,
O'er a' the ills o' life victorious!

But pleasures are like poppies spread,
You seize the flow'r, its bloom is shed;
Or like the snow falls in the river,
A moment white – then melts for ever;
Or like the Borealis race,
That flit ere you can point their place;
Or like the Rainbow's lovely form
Evanishing amid the storm. –
Nae man can tether Time nor Tide,
The hour approaches Tam maun ride;
That hour, o' night's black arch the key-stane,
That dreary hour he mounts his beast in;
And sic a night he taks the road in,
As ne'er poor sinner was abroad in.

The wind blew as 'twad blawn its last;
The rattling showers rose on the blast;
The speedy gleams the darkness swallow'd;
Loud, deep, and lang, the thunder bellow'd:
That night, a child might understand,
The Deil had business on his hand.

Weel-mounted on his grey mare, Meg,
A better never lifted leg,
Tam skelpit on thro' dub and mire,
Despising wind, and rain, and fire;
Whiles holding fast his gude blue bonnet,
Whiles crooning o'er some auld Scots sonnet,
Whiles glow'rin round wi' prudent cares,
Lest bogles catch him unawares;
Kirk-Alloway was drawing nigh,
Where ghaists and houlets nightly cry.

By this time he was cross the ford,
Where in the snaw the chapman smoor'd;
And past the birks and meikle stane,
Where drunken Charlie brak's neck-bane;
And thro' the whins, and by the cairn,
Where hunters fand the murder'd bairn;
And near the thorn, aboon the well,
Where Mungo's mither hang'd hersel'.
Before him Doon pours all his floods,
The doubling storm roars thro' the woods,
The lightnings flash frae pole to pole,
Near and more near the thunders roll,
When, glimmering thro' the groaning trees,
Kirk-Alloway seem'd in a bleeze,
Thro' ilka bore the beams were glancin',
And loud resounded mirth and dancin'.

Inspiring bold John Barleycorn!
What dangers thou canst make us scorn!
Wi' tippenny, we fear nae evil;
Wi' usquabae, we'll face the devil!
The swats sae ream'd in Tammie's noddle,
Fair play, he car'd na deils a boddle,
But Maggie stood, right sair astonish'd,
Till, by the heel and hand admonish'd,
She ventur'd forward on the light;
And, wow! Tam saw an unco sight!

Warlocks and witches in a dance:
Nae cotillon, brent new frae France,
But hornpipes, jigs, strathspeys, an' reels,
Put life an' mettle in their heels.
A winnock-bunker in the east,
There sat auld Nick, in shape o' beast;

A towzie tyke, black, grim, and large,
To gie them music was his charge:
He screw'd the pipes and gart them skirl,
Till roof and rafters a' did dirl.
Coffins stood round, like open presses,
That shaw'd the Dead in their last dresses;
And (by some devilish cantraip sleight)
Each in its cauld hand held a light.
By which heroic Tam was able
To note upon the haly table,
A murderer's banes, in gibbet-airns;
Twa span-lang, wee, unchristened bairns;
A thief, new-cutted frae a rape,
Wi' his last gasp his gab did gape;
Five tomahawks, wi' blude red-rusted:
Five scimitars, wi' murder crusted;
A garter which a babe had strangled:
A knife, a father's throat had mangled.
Whom his ain son of life bereft,
The grey-hairs yet stack to the heft;
Wi' mair of horrible and awfu',
Which even to name wad be unlawfu'.
Three lawyers' tongues, turned inside out,
Wi' lies seam'd like a beggar's clout;
Three priests' tongues, rotten, black as muck,
Lay stinking in every neuk.

As Tammie glowr'd, amaz'd, an' curious,
The mirth and fun grew fast an' furious;
The Piper loud an' louder blew,
The dancers quick an' quicker flew,
The reel'd, they set, they cross'd, they cleekit,

Till ilka carlin swat an' reekit,
An' coost her duddies to the wark,
An' linkit at it in her sark!

Now Tam, O Tam! had they been queans,
A' plump an' strapping in their teens!
Their sarks, instead o' creeshie flannen,
Been snaw-white seventeen hunder linen! –
Thir breeks o' mine, my only pair,
That ance were plush o' guid blue hair,
I wad hae gien them off my hurdies,
For ae blink o' the bonie burdies!
But wither'd beldams, auld and droll,
Rigwoodie hags wad spean a foal,
Louping an' flinging on a crummock.
I wonder didna turn thy stomach.

But Tam kent what was what fu' brawlie:
There was ae winsome wench and waulie
That night enlisted in the core,
Lang after ken'd on Carrick shore;
(For mony a beast to dead she shot,
And perish'd mony a bonie boat,
And shook baith meikle corn and bear,
And kept the country-side in fear);
Her cutty sark, o' Paisley harn,
That while a lassie she had worn,
In longitude tho' sorely scanty,
It was her best, and she was vauntie.
Ah! Little ken'd thy reverend grannie,
That sark she coft for her wee Nannie,
Wi twa pund Scots ('twas a' her riches),
Wad ever grac'd a dance of witches!

But here my Muse her wing maun cour,
Sic flights are far beyond her power;
To sing how Nannie lap and flang,
(A souple jade she was and strang),
And how Tam stood, like ane bewitch'd,
And thought his very een enrich'd:
Even Satan glowr'd, and fidg'd fu' fain,
And hotch'd and blew wi' might and main:
Till first ae caper, syne anither,
Tam tint his reason a thegither,
And roars out, 'Weel done, Cutty-sark!'
And in an instant all was dark:
And scarcely had he Maggie rallied,
When out the hellish legion sallied.

As bees bizz out wi' angry fyke,
When plundering herds assail their byke;
As open pussie's mortal foes,
When, pop! She starts before their nose;
As eager runs the market-crowd,
When 'Catch the thief!' resounds aloud;
So Maggie runs, the witches follow,
Wi' mony an eldritch skreich and hollow.

Ah, Tam! Ah, Tam! thou'll get thy fairin'!
In hell, they'll roast thee like a herrin'!
In vain thy Kate awaits thy comin'!
Kate soon will be a woefu' woman!
Now, do thy speedy-utmost, Meg,
And win the keystane o' the brig;
There, at them thou thy tail may toss,
A running stream they dare na cross.
But ere the keystane she could make,
The fient a tail she had to shake!

For Nannie, far before the rest,
Hard upon noble Maggie prest,
And flew at Tam wi' furious ettle;
But little wist she Maggie's mettle!
Ae spring brought off her master hale,
But left behind her ain grey tail:
The carlin claught her by the rump,
And left poor Maggie scarce a stump.

Now, wha this tale o' truth shall read,
Ilk man and mother's son, take heed:
Whene'er to Drink you are inclin'd,
Or Cutty-sarks rin in your mind,
Think ye may buy the joys o'er dear;
Remember Tam o' Shanter's mare.

[It is a well-known fact that witches, or any evil spirits, have no power to follow a poor wight any further than the middle of the next running stream. It may be proper likewise to mention to the benighted traveller, that when he falls in with bogles, whatever danger may be in his going forward, there is much more hazard in turning back. – RB]

Appendix V

Some Apposite Quotations

I thought that it would help arrangers of Burns Suppers to have some good quotes to use on menu cards or invitations, but these could equally well be used by the chairman as introductions, or to flavour a speech.

Parts of The Supper

The Opening	'From scenes like these old Scotia's grandeur springs, That makes her loved at home, revered abroad: Princes and lords are but the breath of Kings, An honest man's the noblest work of God.'
Grace	'They never sought in vain that sought the Lord aright'
The Food	'The Chief of Scotia's food'
'Address to a Haggis'	'Great chieftain o' the pudding race'
The Addresser	'But mark the Rustic, Haggis fed The very earth resounds his tread' 'Poor wretch, see him ow'er his trash'

The Piper	'Auld Caledon drew out her drone,
	  And to her pipe was singing, O:
	'Twas Pibroch, Sang, Strathspeys, and Reels,
	  She dirl'd them aff fu' clearly, O:'

Wines	'I was'na fu' I just had plenty' 'Go fetch to me a pint o' wine'

Whisky	'Freedom and Whisky gang thegither'
	'Wi' usquebae, we'll face the devil!'
The Chairman	'I am a keeper of the law In some sma' points, altho' not a"
The Immortal Memory	'Perhaps it may turn out a sang, Perhaps turn out a sermon'
The Lassies	'Then gently scan your brother man, Still gentler sister woman'
	'And let us mind, faint heart ne'er wan A lady fair; Wha does the utmost that he can, Will whyles do mair.'
	'The wisest man the warl' saw, He dearly lov'd the lassies O.'

The Reply/ The Laddies	'Auld nature swears, the lovely dears,
	   Her noblest work she classes O;
	Her prentice han' she tried on Man,
	   An' then she made the Lassies O.'

The Guests	'An there's a hand my trusty fiere, An' gie's a hand o' thine'
Absent Friends	'But aye the tear comes in my ee, To think of him that's far awa.'
Singers (Female)	'In ev'ry glen the mavis sang, All nature list'ning seem'd the while'
Community Singing	'See the smoking bowl before us! Mark our jovial, ragged ring! Round and round take up the chorus, And in raptures let us sing'

Musicians	'Hale be your heart, hale be your fiddle, Lang may your elbuck jink an' diddle, To cheer you thro' the weary widdle 　　　O' war'ly cares'
The Company	'Contented wi' little and cantie wi' mair.' 'We are na fou, we're nae that fou, But just a drappie in our ee.'
The End	'Nae man can tether time or tide'

Occupations

Taxman or Customs Officer	'The Deil's awa' wi' the Exciseman'
Gentleman	'A gentleman who held the patent for his honours immediately from Almighty God'
Teacher	'What's a' your jargon of the schools, If honest nature made you fools'
Soldier or Serviceman	'I am a son of Mars, who have been in many wars' 'My humble knapsack a' may wealth, A puir but honest sodger'
Banker	'Gie wealth to some be-ledgered cit, 　　In cent. per cent.; But give me real, sterling wit, 　　And I'm content'
Doctor	'And then, a' doctor's saws an' whittles, Of a' dimensions, shapes, an' mettles, A' kind o' boxes, mugs, an' bottles, 　　　He's sure to hae; Their Latin names as fast he rattles 　　　As A B C.'

Dentist	'My curse upon your venom'd stang, That shoots my tortur'd gooms alang'

Minister of Religion	'Hear how he clears the poits o' Faith
	  Wi' rattlin and thumpin!
	Now meekly calm, now wild in wrath,
	  He's stampin', an' he's jumpin'!'

Politician	'Suppose I take a spurt, and mix Amang the wilds o' politics –' 'Sic a parcel o' rogues in the nation'
Clothes	'Here some are thinkin' on their sins, An' some upon their claes'
Student	'Leese me on drink! It gies us mair Than either school or college.'
Highlander	'My heart's in the Highlands, my heart is not here'
Journalist	'If there's a hole in a' your coats I rede you tent it: There's a chiel amang you taking notes, And, faith, he'll prent it'
Innkeeper or Hotelier	'The landlord's laugh was ready chorus'

Brewer or Publican	'O had the malt thy strength of mind,
	  Or hops the flavour of thy wit,
	'Twere drink for first of human kind,
	  A gift that e'en for thee were fit.'

Farmer	'My father was a farmer upon the Carrick border, O, And carefully he bred me in decency and order, O'

Freemason	'Then fill up a bumper and make it o'erflow, And honours masonic prepare for to throw; May ev'ry true Brother of the Compass and Square Have a big-belly'd bottle when harass'd with care'
Lawyer	'But what his common sense came short, He eked out wi' law, man'
Judge	'The Bench sae wise lift up their eyes, Hauf-waukene'd wi' the din, man.'
From Ayr	'Auld Ayr, wham ne'er a toon surpasses For honest men and bonnie lasses'
From Edinburgh	'Thy sons, Edina, social, kind, With open arms the stranger hail'
From America	'But come ye sons of Liberty, Columbia's offspring, brave as free'
From England	'And England triumphant display her proud rose'

Cheeky Comments

'A wretch, a villain, lost to love and truth'

'Down flow'd her robe, a tartan sheen,
Till half a leg was scrimply seen'

'There's some are fou o' love divine,
There's some are fou o' brandy'

'Partly wi' love overcome sae sair,
An partly she was drunk'

'His ancient, trusty drouthy crony'

But don't just use these – read the poems yourself! Whatever you choose to do – enjoy yourself as RB would want you to!